MODERN WORLD NATIONS

Iraq

Dale Lightfoot
Oklahoma State University

Series Editor
Charles F. Gritzner
South Dakota State University

CHELSEA HOUSE
P U B L I S H E R S
An imprint of Infobase Publishing

Frontispiece: Flag of Iraq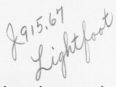

Cover: Sunni Muslims help themselves to candy outside Um al-Qura Mosque in Baghdad, Iraq, during the holiday of Eid al-Fitr.

Iraq

Copyright © 2007 by Infobase Publishing

Chelsea House
An imprint of Infobase Publishing
132 West 31st Street
New York NY 10001

Library of Congress Cataloging-in-Publication Data

Lightfoot, Dale.
    Iraq / Dale Lightfoot.
        p. cm. — (Modern world nations)
    Includes bibliographical references and index.
    ISBN 0-7910-9247-X (hardcover)
 1. Iraq—Juvenile literature. I. Title. II. Series.
 DS70.62.L54 2006
 956.7—dc22   2006012725

Chelsea House books are available at special discounts when purchased in bulk quantities for businesses, associations, institutions, or sales promotions. Please call our Special Sales Department in New York at (212) 967-8800 or (800) 322-8755.

You can find Chelsea House on the World Wide Web at http://www.chelseahouse.com

Series and cover design by Takeshi Takahashi

Printed in the United States of America

Bang Hermitage 10 9 8 7 6 5 4 3 2 1

This book is printed on acid-free paper.

All links and Web addresses were checked and verified to be correct at the time of publication. Because of the dynamic nature of the Web, some addresses and links may have changed since publication and may no longer be valid.

Table of Contents

MODERN WORLD NATIONS

Iraq

Introducing Iraq

Mesopotamia . . . Babylon . . . Saddam . . . Gulf War. From the beginnings of Western Civilization to the present day, events in Iraq have been at the center of world change. Iraq lies in the middle of the Middle East and is central to this important region in countless ways. The domestication of many plants and animals first began here. The world's first urban settlements and civilization originated in Iraq. The hanging gardens of Babylon—one of the original "seven wonders of the world"—added to the fame of this historic center of Arab and Islamic art, architecture, science, and power. Modern Iraq remains an important Arab heartland, but minority groups—especially the Kurds of northern Iraq—are shaping the character of a new multiethnic federal Iraq.

THE PLACE

Iraq (Arabic for "mud bank" or "cliff") lies in a region known as the Middle East, because it is east of Europe. The term *Middle East* is

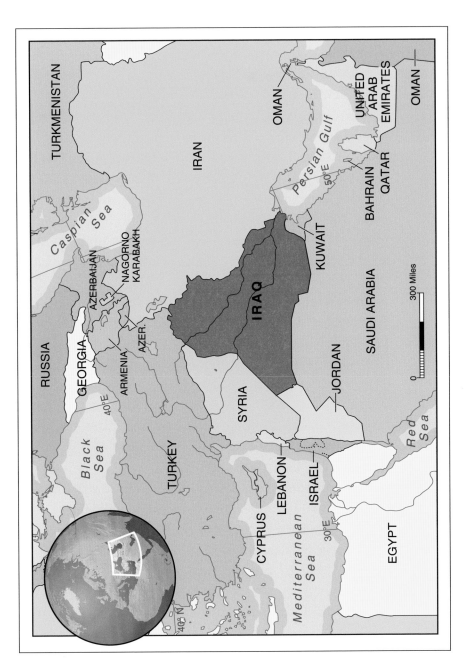

Iraq is located in the Middle East and shares borders with six countries: Iran, Jordan, Kuwait, Saudi Arabia, Syria, and Turkey. Although Iraq's climate is quite arid, the country is watered by the Tigris and Euphrates rivers, which flow through the heart of the country.

drawn from a European perspective. But it is commonly used around the world to distinguish this region from the *Far East,* or lands of eastern Asia. Geographically, the region can also be called Southwest Asia.

Iraq lies in a region often called the "Dry World." This is because a huge area of desert stretches across North Africa, the Middle East, and Central Asia. But neither the Middle East nor Iraq is all dry. Most Iraqis live where there is water. They are clustered in the mountains of the Kurdish northeast, or in the broad Tigris-Euphrates river basin that runs the length of the country from north to south. The Tigris and Euphrates rivers are the country's lifelines. Their waters begin as snow melt in the high mountains of eastern Turkey. The streams then flow southward for 1,000 miles across semiarid and arid regions of Syria and Iraq, bringing water and life to areas that would be far less livable without these great rivers. For the last 100 miles, the rivers join together in a flat, marshy wetland called the Shatt al-Arab, which carries the combined river flow into the Persian Gulf. Part of the Shatt al-Arab waterway forms the boundary between Iraq and Iran. Iraq's only coastline is about 19 miles (30 kilometers) long, situated where the Shatt al-Arab water-way flows into the Persian Gulf.

Most of western Iraq is parched, almost lifeless, desert. This region, part of the Arabian-Syrian Desert, is the country's most sparsely populated region. Iraq lies in an area of the world where water is often scarce, vegetation scant, and population sparse. Water, good agricultural land, and other essential resources are relatively abundant, however, in the parts of the country where most people live.

Baghdad, Iraq's capital and largest city, lies near the center of the country. Other large, important cities include Basra in the far south (near Kuwait), and Kirkuk and Mosul in the north. Baghdad is an ethnically mixed city and has served as the administrative and cultural heart of the region since the time of ancient Babylon (about 1700 B.C.). Basra is a mostly Shia (sect of Islam) Arab city, and lies in one of the two most important oil-producing areas of Iraq. The other big oil-producing region is around Kirkuk, in northeastern Iraq, along the boundary between Arab and Kurdish areas of Iraq.

THE PEOPLE

Iraq is part of the "Arab World," the huge region that spans much of North Africa and the Middle East in which Arabic is the dominant language. Most people in Iraq are Arabs, though a Turkomen (Turkish) minority and a large Kurdish population make up most of the people in northeastern Iraq. Because it has long been a center of regional power and influence, and most of the population is Arab, the country has been politically active in the Arab World since it became an independent state in 1932.

Another name given to the region is the "Islamic World," because most people here are Muslims (someone who practices the Islamic faith). The founder of the Islamic faith, the prophet Muhammad, was born in nearby Arabia in A.D. 571. In the centuries after Muhammad's death in 632, Islam spread into portions of Africa, Asia, and Europe by means of Islamic conquest and trade. Islam was the religion of Arab merchants and the military, and these travelers carried it with them wherever they journeyed. Most people in Iraq are Muslim, including most Arabs, Kurds, and Turkomen. About 3 percent of the population is Christian.

Iraq is one of only three countries in the Middle East where the Shia branch of Islam is the majority faith (the others being Iran and Bahrain). Most Shia Arabs here are concentrated in southern Iraq. Sunni Arabs, mostly in the center of Iraq, make up less than a third of the population. Though there are almost twice as many Shia as there are Sunni Muslims in Iraq, Sunni Muslims have been the leaders of the territory since the beginning of Iraq's Islamic history in the seventh century. In some countries, the Sunni-Shia distinction is not very noticeable. But in Iraq, a Shia majority has been politically dominated by a Sunni minority for a very long time, and openly persecuted for almost 25 years under the government of Saddam Hussein. In Iraq, the Sunni-Shia divide among the Arab population plays a pivotal role in political and social relations. It has even been a major stumbling block in the search for a workable federal constitution to govern a new Iraq. Like the Sunni Arabs, the Kurds are mostly Sunni Muslim, but they are not natural allies of the Sunni Arabs. In the recent post-Saddam era, Kurdish politicians favor a secular (nonreligious) government and a high degree of Kurdish autonomy (if not independence) within a federal Iraqi state.

The core of Iraq, centered in Baghdad, and the Shia Arab-dominated south, are two of Iraq's major subregions. A third subregion lies in the north—the land of the Kurds. The Kurds make up as much as 20 percent of the country's population. Iraq's Kurds occupy an important area of the country, because the huge oil reserves around the city of Kirkuk lie partly in Kurdish territory.

Iraq has a population estimated at approximately 27 million, or about one-tenth that of the United States. Because of its major oil reserves and large areas of irrigated farmland, Iraq has more abundant natural resources than many of its neighbors. Descended from the early Mesopotamian states and empires that emerged in the basin of the Tigris and Euphrates rivers, Iraq also has a rich history.

ORIGINS AND EVOLUTION OF TERRITORY

Since the times of earliest human history, the abundance of resources in the core of Iraq has made the area an attractive place for settlement. The region has been home to some of the world's greatest civilizations. For example, the ancient civilizations of Sumer, Assyria, and Babylon developed in Mesopotamia—the land between the Tigris and Euphrates rivers in present-day Iraq. Over the past 2,500 years, the area

Baghdad, Iraq's largest city and capital, lies on the Tigris River in the center of the country. Pictured here is Firdos Square in central Baghdad. A statue of former President Saddam Hussein, which was toppled in 2003, can be seen on the right side of the square.

has been contested and occupied by Persians (Iran), Greeks, Arabs, and Turks.

For most of its history, Iraq remained a powerful core territory within these larger empires. In fact, it was not recognized by its present name or current borders until the early twentieth century, when the British briefly took control of the area. The British, who inherited this territory from the Ottoman Turks—the defeated allies of Germany in World War I—saw the potential value of Iraq's oil resources. When they drew territorial (political) boundaries, they made certain to include the area's fields of "black gold." Most of the oil fields are concentrated in the far south, where Shia Arabs are the majority population, and in the far north, where the Kurdish population lives. The Sunni Arabs in between were politically joined to the Kurds and Shia Arabs. They occupied the gap between the oil fields, and also the famous and important city of Baghdad that lay in the center of the new country. Iraqi kings and presidents, who have ruled Iraq since the British departed in 1932, inherited these borders. The most famous of these recent rulers—the dictator Saddam Hussein—was removed from power during a British- and U.S.-led invasion and occupation of Iraq in 2003. Saddam Hussein was a central figure in Iraq's conflicts with its neighboring countries.

CONFLICTS WITH NEIGHBORING COUNTRIES

Before 1923, the Iraq we recognize today had no neighboring countries. It was part of much larger empires that at various times were controlled by Assyrians, Persians, Greeks, Arabs, and Turks. The Mesopotamian core was usually at or near the center of each empire; conflicts with neighbors occurred far away at the edge of these expansive empires. Iraq is now bordered by six neighboring countries and has experienced disagreements with most of them. Two of these disagreements led to war, and one of these wars led eventually to the overthrow of Saddam Hussein. Saddam was president of Iraq from 1979 to 2003, during which time he was a frequent menace to his neighbors.

To the west, the country adjoins Jordan and Syria. Jordan maintains good relations with Iraq, and most Iraqis today look favorably upon Jordanians (and vice versa). When Iraq's only seaport near Basra was closed during the Iran-Iraq war of the 1980s, Jordan allowed Iraq to ship its oil through the country, so the Iraqi economy would not be crippled. Jordan again provided Iraq with an outlet to the sea through the port of Aqaba during the 1991 Gulf War. Relations between Jordan and Iraq have sometimes been strained, but not to the extent that they have been with most of Iraq's other neighbors.

In the mid-twentieth century, Syria and Iraq were political allies. But when Saddam Hussein rose to power in 1979, that relationship degraded into one of fierce competition, and not only in the political arena. The Euphrates River passes through Syria before it enters Iraq. After the Syrians built a dam on the river in the early 1970s, they began impounding and using water (particularly for irrigation) that previously flowed into Iraq. Water is always a potential source of heated conflict in this arid zone.

Turkey lies to the north and both the Tigris and Euphrates originate in the country's snowy eastern mountains. Today, the Turks are in the midst of an ambitious program to build 22 dams on the upper Tigris and Euphrates rivers. This has degraded relations between Turkey and Iraq.

To the east of Iraq lies Iran, a country that Saddam Hussein invaded in 1980. This led to a devastating, decade-long war during the 1980s. This conflict followed a long period of dispute between Iran and Iraq over control of the Shatt al-Arab waterway. Iran and Iraq also disagreed over rights to oil production and refining in the region, and the location of the international boundary that divides the area's mostly Arab population.

At the head of the Persian Gulf lies Kuwait, a country invaded by Iraq's army in 1990. Several major oil fields are found in the Shatt al-Arab between the city of Basra and Kuwait. One, the Rumailah oil field, extends from beneath Iraqi soil into Kuwait. In 1990, Iraq claimed that Kuwait was drilling oil from this field by using slanted wells under Iraqi territory. Iraq also claimed that the boundary between the two countries was never agreed upon. The Shatt al-Arab waterway was still choked with the wreckage of the recent Iran-Iraq War. Annexation of Kuwait would also give Iraq a new outlet to the Persian Gulf. The desire for more land, more oil, and more seacoast persuaded Iraq to invade and occupy its southern neighbor. Kuwait was liberated by a U.S.–led international force in 1991, but the instigator of the invasion—Saddam Hussein— remained in power and relations with Kuwait remained very poor. With a new political administration now taking shape in Iraq, diplomatic relations with Kuwait have improved, though Iraqi-Kuwaiti relations remain strained.

To the south lies Saudi Arabia, which (like Jordan) assisted Iraq with the shipment of its oil supplies in the 1980s, but broke from Iraq after the invasion of Kuwait in 1990. Saudi Arabia felt directly threatened by that invasion, and the Saudis played a key role in the international effort that removed Iraqi forces from Kuwait in 1991. They also played an important role in Gulf War II (2003) that removed Saddam Hussein from power in Iraq.

PRESENT AND FUTURE OF IRAQ

Iraq is a country in transition, and its future is uncertain. On the positive side, the dictator Saddam Hussein and his Baathist (political party) government were removed from power during the U.S.–led invasion during Gulf War II. However, disagreements between Sunni Arabs, Shia Arabs, and Kurds were held in check by Saddam's tightfisted control. On the negative side, they are now free to bicker amongst one another. In the new Iraq, these groups are challenged by the task of trying to find new ways of cooperation and living peaceably together.

Iraq has long been an economic and political powerhouse in the Middle East. By the 1970s, the country had one of the best road networks, best health-care systems, and best public-school and university systems in the Middle East. It was a rapidly modernizing and industrializing country, well funded by a growing oil industry, and protected by one of the world's largest military forces. Unfortunately for ordinary Iraqis, their political leadership squandered that wealth and power on themselves. Saddam Hussein, his family, and his closest supporters siphoned off much of the country's wealth. They enjoyed some of the world's most lavish lifestyles and felt the need to pay for an army that protected themselves and constantly threatened their neighbors.

Much of Iraq's potential was wasted on the earlier conflict with Iran. Its infrastructure (for example, bridges, roads, power supplies, schools) and economy were further damaged during the first Gulf War (1991) and shattered during the second Gulf War (2003). Iraq is blessed with water, good land for farming, and large oil reserves. Without the glaring mismanagement, corruption, and inefficiency of the Saddam Hussein government, Iraq would have been one of the region's best economic success stories. Instead, its botched leadership made it one of the world's saddest tragedies. The country suffered enormously from the problems brought about by three wars in three decades. Saddam Hussein also failed to comply fully with agreements he made to end the invasion of his country during the first Gulf War. This brought about a decade of economic sanctions that plunged the country into further poverty and despair. Desperately needed relief has been coming in from many countries since the U.S.–led invasion of Iraq that toppled Saddam Hussein in 2003.

In many ways, Iraq's slate has been wiped clean. Sanctions have ended, and many countries have poured billions of dollars into the country. Electrical energy is being redeveloped and the oil industry is being expanded to generate more money for the country. Schools have been resupplied and universities have new technologies for teaching and research that had been denied them during more than a decade of sanctions. Most of the country received Internet service for the first time in 2004 and the public now has access to the World Wide Web (though relatively few people outside of universities or the government have computers). Political and religious persecution and torture

Former Iraqi president Saddam Hussein, pictured here in 1995, waves to supporters in Baghdad. Hussein served as president of Iraq from 1979 until he was removed from power by a U.S.–led coalition during the second Gulf War in 2003.

are no longer used to maintain law and order. A free press and free civil society is slowly evolving.

Yet there is more trouble ahead for Iraq. The speed of political change, and the violent nature of that change, has created a power vacuum and instability that did not exist before. Though Iraq frequently invaded its neighbors, or made them feel threatened, its neighbors are not threatening Iraq. However, the lack of internal security remains a real threat. In 2006, a civil insurgency continued to fight those trying to develop and restore order to the country. Some of these insurgents are religious extremists opposed to non-Muslim (U.S. and British) invasion and influence in the country. Some insurgents are

Sunni Arabs who are angry at their loss of power and angry at the United States for upstaging them. Political disagreements between Sunni and Shia Arabs over the rules of government, and Kurdish demands for greater independence from Arab control, all confound a delicate balance of power in the new Iraq. These internal conflicts cloud the positive accomplishments on other fronts.

2

Physical Landscapes

The physical environment is more than just a collection of deserts, rivers, mountains, and climate. Physical features help to define the character of the land and describe the benefits or constraints to development faced by the people who live in this landscape. The physical environment provides the natural setting in which the human drama of the Middle East takes place.

It is tempting to characterize Iraq's physical environment in a few words by focusing on the dryness of the region. But most of the country's people live where there is water—around the Tigris and Euphrates rivers and in the hills and mountains of northern Iraq. We could characterize this country as one where water is sometimes limited, but water and other natural resources are available for human development.

RIVERS

The ancient name for the heart of Iraq is *Mesopotamia*—"land between the rivers." The two rivers are the Tigris and Euphrates—the economic lifeblood of Iraq. These rivers were responsible for the development of the world's first agricultural societies and first urban civilizations. Flowing through an otherwise dry region, they are central to the physical and human geography of Iraq. The rivers run through the geographic center of the country, and political, economic, and cultural activities in Iraq remain centered around them.

The Tigris River originates in Turkey before flowing into Iraq. The Euphrates also begins in Turkey, but flows through Syria before entering the country. The rivers meet at al-Qurnah, in southern Iraq, forming the combined waterway known as the Shatt al-Arab, which then flows into the Persian Gulf. This waterway forms a portion of the boundary between Iran and Iraq.

The Tigris River is narrower than the Euphrates, but it carries more water. Both rivers have been used as water highways since ancient times. Still, they create problems for modern transportation. The lower sections of the rivers often flood, which hinders road building. The fast currents of the upper sections prevent boats from traveling upstream. The rivers are wide and slow near the Persian Gulf, but are also very shallow. Dredging (use of a machine to deepen the water bed) has been necessary to allow shipping in these waters.

THE LAND

Iraq is a land of varied physical landscapes. There are vast desert plains and rugged plateaus. Mountainous terrain adds to the country's environmental diversity and land-use potentials.

Plains and Plateaus

The low plain of southern Mesopotamia begins north of Baghdad and extends to the Persian Gulf. Most of Iraq's people live

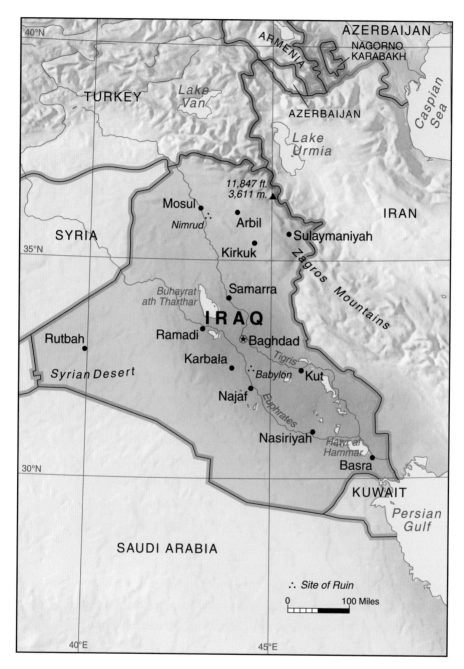

Much of Iraq consists of desert plains and rugged plateaus; however, the area between the Tigris and Euphrates rivers is very fertile. In addition, the northern part of the country is very mountainous, with several peaks over 10,000 feet (3,048 meters).

in and around this palm-covered, subtropical plain. The plain is alluvial (stream-deposited sediment)—built up by the mud and sand laid down by the rivers. Large quantities of mineral salts also are carried by the rivers. Due to the high water table and poor drainage, these salts concentrate near the surface, damaging crops and limiting successful farming. The Mesopotamian plain contains many archaeological sites, including ancient Babylon (south of Baghdad), and the ancient ruins of Ur and Kish, possibly the world's first cities.

The great alluvial plain of Mesopotamia ends in a large delta—flat, alluvial land where stream-carried sediments build up as the river meets the sea. River-deposited silt is building up the delta's plain at a rate of about eight inches every 100 years. The delta land is grooved by meandering river channels and straight irrigation canals. Temporary lakes form when the rivers flood.

In the south, near Basra, a large part of the delta was once a swampy region inhabited by Arabs living in reed houses. At the end of Gulf War I (1991), Saddam Hussein built a large canal to drain the marshes and divert the water to desert land. This was done in part to destroy rebel bases hidden in the marshland. Residents of the area—the Marsh Arabs (or *Madan*)—had to flee for safety across the border to Iran.

The rolling landscape between the Tigris River (north of Samarra) and the Euphrates River (north of Ramadi) is called al-Jazirah (the island). This broad grassland plateau of northern Mesopotamia has a semiarid climate, much like the Great Plains of the central United States. Here, the water has cut deep valleys into the land, which makes irrigation difficult. However, rain-fed agriculture is possible in the region, and wheat, barley, and similar grains are grown. The Jazirah region contains many archaeological remains, including the ancient city of Assur, center of the ancient Assyrian Empire.

Beyond the fertile plains and plateaus, the country changes to vast, dry desert in the west and to a cold, mountainous landscape in the north.

Deserts

The western third of Iraq is barren desert. This desolate region is part of the Syrian Desert that stretches westward into Syria and Jordan, and southward to cover much of the Arabian Peninsula. The desert is flat, rocky, and sparsely vegetated.

Iraq's western desert is the most sparsely populated area of the country, because there is little water and the land is parched. The desert plain is etched with *wadis*—stream channels that are dry most of the year. During the winter season, however, rain sends dangerous flash floods through these intermittent stream beds. In the spring, after winter showers have watered the surface, the desert areas often develop a thick cover of short-lived flowering plants. As quickly as the carpet of plant life arrives, the vegetation vanishes, giving way to barren land for the rest of the year.

Mountains

Most of Iraq's land surface is lower than 1,000 feet (300 meters) above sea level. Only 15 percent of the land—in the northern foothills and mountains—is above 1,500 feet (450 meters) in elevation. This rugged, mountainous region is inhabited mainly by the Kurds, a non-Arab people. The Zagros Mountains rise in northeastern Iraq and extend into Iran. This range has many peaks above 9,000 feet (2,740 meters). The highest peaks are near Iraq's borders with Turkey and Iran, including a snowy, unnamed peak (the highest in Iraq) at 11,844 feet (3,611 meters) and Haji Ibrahim at 11,834 feet (3,607 meters). These high, snow-covered peaks surround valleys in which the Kurds cultivate their crops and tend to their livestock.

This mountainous zone contains some of Iraq's richest mineral deposits. Transportation in the rugged highlands has never been as reliable as in the warmer and flatter parts of the country. The mountains also have a cool and temperate climate, unlike the hotter parts of the country to the south. Kurdish inhabitants of these highlands have adapted well to the climatic conditions of a longer winter and shorter growing season. Their crops, houses, and clothing, for example, are quite different from those occurring on the hotter and more arid desert plains.

WEATHER AND CLIMATE

Iraq's climate varies greatly from place to place within the country and some annual variation in rainfall and temperature can be expected within any region. In general, Iraq has two very different climatic provinces: (1) the hot, arid lowlands, including the alluvial plains and the deserts; and (2) the cool and moist northeast, where the higher elevations produce lower temperatures and help intercept moisture that falls as summer rain and winter snow. The semi-arid Jazirah Plateau in northern Mesopotamia lies between these two extremes. In the northeast mountains, and in the Jazirah region, rain-fed cultivation is possible. In the hot lowlands, farmers must irrigate the land.

People of the lowlands experience two seasons, dry summer and moist winter, with a short transitional period in between. In summer, which lasts from May to October, there are clear skies, extremely high temperatures, and low relative humidity. Very little, if any, rain falls from June through September. In Baghdad, July and August bring daily temperatures of about 95°F (35°C), and summer afternoon highs can reach 123°F (50°C). Temperatures vary considerably between day and night during the summer. Winter in the lowlands lasts from December to February. Temperatures are generally mild, although extremes of hot and cold, including frosts, can occur. Winter temperature extremes in Baghdad vary between 35° and 60°F (about 1°C and 15°C).

During winter, the paths of west-to-east-moving storm systems cross the Middle East, shift southward, and bring rain to southern Iraq. Annual amounts vary greatly from year to year, but average annual rainfall in the lowlands ranges from four to seven inches (about 1.5 to 3 centimeters). About 90 percent of the rainfall occurs between November and April.

Rain can be a problem as well as a gift in the desert areas. A few days of steady rain can turn dirt roads into thick mud and disrupt mail and telephone service. Planted crops may be washed out. Houses and roofs made of adobe (clay) can leak badly and even erode.

Summer in the northeast uplands is shorter than in the lowlands—from June to September—and the winter lasts longer. The summer is generally dry and hot, but average temperatures are about 5 to 10 degrees cooler than those in lowland Iraq. Cold winters sometimes occur as a result of the higher elevations and the influence of northeasterly winds that bring frigid air from Central Asia. January temperatures in Mosul, which is in the foothills, range from 24° to 63°F (-4°C to 17°C), but temperatures as low as 12°F (-11°C) have been recorded. The higher mountains experience even greater temperature extremes.

Annual rainfall in the foothills of northeastern Iraq ranges from 12 to 22 inches (30.5 to 56 centimeters), enough to sustain a good seasonal pasture. Precipitation may exceed 40 inches (102 centimeters) in the mountains, much of which falls as winter snow. As in the lowlands, little rain falls during the summer. Because of the rugged terrain, mountain rain is useful for the cultivation of crops only in the valleys. In the valleys, foothills, and plains, agriculture is possible without irrigation. But even here, a shortage of rain can lead to crop failure. Because of the long winter and brief summer growing season, only one crop a year can be grown.

All of Iraq is affected by the *shamal*, a steady northerly or northwesterly wind. It is strongest in the winter but occurs year-round. It brings such dry air that hardly any clouds form, permitting intensive heating of the land surface by the sun. This wind often generates dust storms and sandstorms two or three times per month during the winter season.

The *shamal*, a steady northerly/northwesterly wind affects Iraq year-round, but it is particularly damaging during the winter months, when it often generates sandstorms. Pictured here is downtown Baghdad, which has been engulfed by dust during a sandstorm in March 2006.

Another wind, the *sharki*, blows from the south or southeast during early summer and early winter. The sharki may also be accompanied by dust and sandstorms, especially in the desert, where vegetation cover is sparse. Sandstorms may occur in Iraq throughout the year, but are more frequent in the summer. Typically, the worst month is July, when five or six storms may strike central Iraq. The dust in these storms may rise to several thousand feet.

FLORA AND FAUNA

The Mesopotamian plain of Iraq appears lush and green in areas where irrigation allows agriculture. In some places, palm-tree vegetation gives the appearance of a forest. More than 30 million date palms grow in the Mesopotamian plain of Iraq. Orange and lemon trees are also grown in central and southern Iraq. In the absence of irrigation, however, the natural vegetation in most of Iraq is either very sparse or absent.

Vegetation in the rolling grasslands of the Jazirah region—between the northern Tigris and Euphrates rivers—is a mixture of grasses and scattered, low-growing shrubs that live throughout the year and are able to survive the severe heat. In the spring, bright flowering annuals spring to life after receiving moisture from winter rains.

Vast stands of oak once covered the northern Kurdish mountains. Some of these forests have disappeared over the years, because they have been cut down for use as firewood and charcoal. Some oak forest remains and other areas are covered by stands of trees such as pine and maple. Unfortunately, no forestry policies exist to prevent cutting of the remaining trees. Pasturelands in the mountains remain in reasonably good condition, and nomadic herding of sheep and goats is a common activity in these highland pastures.

Throughout the plains, common vegetation includes rockroses, sedges, boxthorns, and rough grasses. In the spring, daisies, buttercups, and poppies thrive. Around villages and cities, date palms, orange and pear trees, rubber plants, and eucalyptus (a hardy species introduced from Australia) are common. Thickets of tamarisk and bulrushes grow along the riverbanks and marshlands, as well as poplar and willow trees.

As in American deserts of Arizona or New Mexico, the deserts of Iraq are mostly devoid of vegetation. However, some desert flora such as rockrose and storksbill survive the dry summer months and bloom in the spring, after winter rains moisten the desert soil.

The most commonly seen mammals in Iraq are domesticated varieties of camels, sheep, and goats. These animals are

Traditionally, Kurdish people, such as the shepherds pictured here with their flock of sheep in northern Iraq, were nomadic and herded domesticated animals in the region's mountains. Today, however, many Kurds live in urban areas and practice farming.

the source of food and livelihood for desert people, and the most popular meats consumed by all Iraqis.

For a country its size, Iraq has relatively little wildlife. Many of its wild creatures, especially in desert areas, appear only at night. Among the most common mammals are deer, mountain goats, jackals, hyenas, wild boars, brown bears, rabbits, bats, wild cats, and squirrels. The lion has become extinct in Iraq, and the ostrich and the wild ass are nearly extinct.

The Tigris and Euphrates contain freshwater fish that are caught for food. Streams and lakes are well stocked with many kinds of fish, notably carp, catfish, and loach. Reptiles abound in the desert areas of Iraq, although lizards are far more numerous than snakes. Some of Iraq's snakes are venomous, such as several varieties of deadly vipers and cobras. Iraq is also a breeding ground for the unwelcome desert locust.

Birds are the most prominent wildlife in Iraq. About 390 species are found throughout the country. Some species of birds stay all year. Many others are migrants and seasonal visitors, some of them attracted by the extensive wetlands of the Shatt al-Arab. Species found in Iraq include crows, European robins, and storks. There are also vultures, buzzards, ravens, owls, and various species of hawks. Birds of prey such as the hawk are sometimes trained for hunting. Other birds include ducks, geese, partridges, and sand grouse.

ENVIRONMENTAL ISSUES

Environmental problems in Iraq have plagued the people of Mesopotamia since ancient times, including poor quality freshwater in some places and salinization of the soil. Salinization occurs when irrigation water cannot properly drain from fields. When pooled irrigation water evaporates at the surface, mineral salts dissolved in the water are left behind. These salts accumulate on, or near, the soil surface until the soil is too salty to produce crops.

The pollution of poverty and war has also degraded the Iraqi environment. As in most developing countries, industrial spills and dumping have accompanied decades of poorly regulated development. Three destructive wars and a decade of economic sanctions further degraded Iraq's environment. The Iran-Iraq War (1980–1988) and the Persian Gulf Wars (1991 and 2003) destroyed wildlife habitat, polluted Iraq's land and water, and led to the neglect of conservation efforts. As previously mentioned, following the first Gulf War, the Saddam Hussein government drained much of the inhabited marsh area of southern Iraq, and diverted streams and rivers that used to flow into the marshes. A large population of Marsh Arabs, who had inhabited the marshes for thousands of years, has been displaced.

During the two Gulf Wars, U.S. forces used tank-busting shells containing depleted uranium. These used shells on the Iraqi landscape have been confirmed as sources of dangerous radioactive dust that can cause kidney disease if ingested, or lung cancer if inhaled. The unreliability of electricity, made worse because of the wars, prevents water pumps from running on a regular schedule. In an attempt to find alternate sources of freshwater, Iraqis have broken underground water pipes and become sick from the untreated water inside.

Much of the equipment and infrastructure for Iraq's resource development was destroyed during the two Gulf Wars, including equipment used in the petroleum industry. To prevent the United States from taking productive wells, Iraq destroyed many oil wells and refineries in southern Iraq at the end of the first Gulf War. This poisoned the air with sulfur dioxide and led to the fallout of other dangerous pollutants. The general lack of environmental regulation in Iraq has led to hazardous wastes being released into the air or dumped into depleted wells.

3

Iraq Through Time

The Republic of Iraq is a young state in a very old land. The birthplace of Western Civilization lies in Iraq's central region of Mesopotamia—"the land between the rivers." The Tigris and Euphrates rivers originate in the highlands of Turkey and flow southward for more than a thousand miles to the Persian Gulf. Along their course they flow past the ruins of cities that stood at the center of the world's first empires. The rivers still flow through a timeless land that has experienced much change, and conflict, in recent history.

MESOPOTAMIA: CULTURAL HEARTH

History, as a written record of human activity and accomplishments, began in Iraq. The historic role of Iraq in world affairs is derived from its central geography. Iraq lies in the center of the Middle East, a region of cultural and economic exchange between Europe, Asia, and Africa, and a hearth and home for world culture.

Important trade goods and new inventions from the Far East—such as silk, sugar, citrus fruit, paper, gunpowder, and the magnetic compass—were introduced to Europe after they were first adopted in the Middle East. Ancient Mesopotamian civilization provided many of its own innovations and inventions to the world. Major contributions include the wheel, advanced irrigation techniques, a system of writing (cuneiform), a calendar, and scientific astronomy. In the soils of the region, plants were first domesticated that are now grown throughout the world, including wheat, rye, barley, peas, beans, grapes, olives, apples, and peaches.

EARLY HISTORY

Civilization—socially complex, urban society with an ability to write—first developed in present-day Iraq. Civilization followed the emergence of a settled agricultural and pastoral way of life. Some 8 to 10 thousand years ago, climate changes at the end of the last ice age led to a decrease of wild game and increase of wild grain. These changes encouraged isolated hill folk and nomadic tribes to settle and stay in one place. They learned to improve tools and farming systems, and the Mesopotamian population increased. As people grew in number, they developed new ways of organizing themselves socially and politically, and rapidly increased the pace of human invention. Many centuries of this social evolution led to the birth of nations, states, and empires.

From the earliest period, the Mesopotamian area was a crossroads for migrating peoples. Between about 5000 B.C. and the time of Christ (A.D. 1), a series of invasions into the area made it a "melting pot" of races and cultures.

The first of the invaders, a Mediterranean people called the Sumerians, established settlements that grew into city-states between the Tigris and Euphrates rivers. Their earliest cities—the first true urban settlements in human history—evolved in Mesopotamia by abut 3200 B.C. (about 5,200 years ago). Sumer was not a unified nation. Each of its separate city-states—including Ur, Erech, Kish, and Laash—maintained local power and influence. These cities traded with one another and grew wealthy from trade to surrounding territories in what would later become Turkey and Iran. The prosperity of these city-states attracted other people from surrounding areas, including the Semitic (Arabic-related) Akkadians who established city-states along the middle Euphrates by about 3000 B.C.

Babylon

For 1,000 years, the Sumerian and Akkadian city-states competed with each other through both trade and warfare. An outside invasion by a common enemy (Elamites from the region that is today western Iran) forced the Sumerians and Akkadians to band together around 1800 B.C. All of Mesopotamia was then unified into the Babylonian Empire, first ruled by Hammurabi of Babylon.

Hammurabi created one of the first written collections of laws in the world, called the Code of Hammurabi. Hammurabi's laws covered issues like property rights, taxes, labor, and family affairs, and served as the foundation for other legal systems in the region. After Hammurabi died, the Babylonian Empire was plundered and weakened by the Hittites (from Asia Minor/Turkey). The Kassites (from the Zagros Mountains) invaded the empire in 1570 B.C. and ruled for another four centuries.

The Assyrians, whose capital lay in the Jazirah region of northern Iraq, began building an empire in the ninth century B.C. that eventually controlled territory from the Mediterranean Sea to the Zagros Mountains of Iran, including part of Babylonia. A rival of the Assyrians—the Chaldeans, who lived in the marshlands of southern Sumer—toppled the Assyrians by 612 B.C. and took control of Babylonia.

The most famous king from the Chaldean era—one of the more famous characters from Iraqi history and someone whom Saddam Hussein admired—was Nebuchadnezzar II (who reigned from 605–562 B.C.). Nebuchadnezzar funded a massive building campaign for Babylon, the empire's capital city. Magnificent palaces and tall temples were built within Babylon's city wall. The famous "Hanging Gardens of Babylon"—one of the seven wonders of the ancient world—were built above Nebuchadnezzar's royal palace. In another section of the city, a new 300-foot (91-meter) tower was dedicated to the god Marduk. This tower is most famously known as the Tower of Babel.

Over the years, disagreements between members of the royal family and clashes with religious leaders weakened Babylonia. This famous Mesopotamian empire was subject to a number of rulers and changing boundaries over the centuries, but continued to exist until 539 B.C. In that year, it was conquered by Persians (from present-day Iran) and absorbed into their larger empire.

Persians and Greeks

There have been several Persian empires through the ages. The first of these to conquer Iraq, and much of the Middle East, was the Achaemenid Empire (in 539 B.C.), led by Cyrus. Cyrus was one of history's great leaders. He ruled with a firm hand, but was also very understanding of his subjects' needs. He replaced the savagery of the Assyrians with respect for the traditions and institutions of the many groups he ruled. His only requirement was that they pay tribute and be obedient to his rule. Still, the Babylonians frequently rebelled against Persian control.

Exploiting these desires to be free of Persian control, the young Greek general Alexander the Great marched his troops into Babylonia in 331 B.C. to force out the Persians. Babylonians welcomed the Greeks as liberators from Persian control. Alexander was a great admirer of Persian art and science, and it was his wish to combine the best elements of Greek and Persian culture. Alexander continued to expand Greek influence across the region until his grand empire stretched from Egypt to Central Asia. After Alexander's death in 323 B.C., his generals fought over control of different parts of the empire. One of these fragments—the Greek Seleucid Dynasty—controlled Mesopotamia for about 200 years and infused the region with Hellenistic (ancient Greek) culture. By 150 B.C., Persians again inherited the Mesopotamian region. These Parthian Persians, and later Sassanid Persians, controlled the area until the Arab conquest swept through the region in the seventh century A.D.

Arabs and Turks

The Arab-Islamic conquest of what is now Iraq started in A.D. 633 and ended in 636 at the Battle of Qadisiyya, a village on the Euphrates River, south of Baghdad. During this battle, an Islamic army defeated Persian forces that were six times larger. The Arab army moved quickly to the capital of the Sassanian Empire, where in 637 it seized the immense Persian treasury. Many tribes in the conquered lands were Christian Arabs. Some of them converted to Islam. Those who didn't convert were free to practice their Christian religion, provided that they pay a tax.

The first Arab Islamic group that controlled Iraq was the Umayyad Empire. This was also the first Islamic empire to establish an inherited monarchy (series of kings) system, so that the king's family would remain in control of the empire. The Umayyad capital was Damascus, in present-day Syria, so Iraq was not the center of the empire. Civil war and corruption from within led to the overthrow of the Umayyads in 747 and establishment of the Abbasid Empire. Under the Abbasids, the capital of the Islamic empire was moved to Baghdad, which served as the center of Islamic power and achievement for 400 years.

This was the Golden Age of growth and achievement for Baghdad, and for the surrounding region of Mesopotamia. The Abbasid period saw Baghdad become the second-largest city in

The northern Iraq city of Samarra is the site of the Al Malwiya Mosque and spiral minaret (pictured here). Built by the Abbasid ruler Al-Mutawakkil in the mid-ninth century A.D., the minaret is unique in that it becomes thinner with height and has an external spiral staircase.

the known world after Constantinople, and the most important center of science and art. The Abbasid realm was a forceful military power. Its borders reached from North Africa in the west to China in the east.

The Abbasid era was a time of great contrasts. On the one hand, there was a real cultural brilliance, with original and lasting works in medicine, astronomy, architecture, and geography. At the same time, there was imperial rot, where spoiled, reckless, self-absorbed *caliphs* (Islamic leaders) allowed the state to decay.

By the mid-ninth century, the Abbasid Empire began a slow decline. Turkic warrior-slaves, known as Mamluks, became so prominent at the king's court that they began to monopolize power. Exploiting this weakness in 945, the Buwayhids, an

Iranian Shia dynasty, conquered Baghdad. In 1055, the Seljuks, a Turkish Sunni clan, conquered the Buwayhids and reestablished Sunni rule in Baghdad. By the end of the eleventh century, Seljuk power started to decline.

Hulagu, a grandson of the great Mongol conqueror Genghis Khan, took control of Baghdad in 1258. He killed all of the scholars and erected a pyramid from their skulls. The sophisticated irrigation system constructed by the Abbasids was destroyed. Iraq became a neglected frontier area ruled from the Mongol capital of Tabriz in Iran. In 1335, the last Mongol ruler of this region died. Further chaos ensued in 1401, when the Turkic conqueror Tamerlane (from what is now Uzbekistan in Central Asia) destroyed Baghdad. He massacred many of the city's inhabitants and his conquest marked the end of Baghdad's prominence.

Over the next few centuries, Ottoman Turks and Iranian Persians—the power centers to the west and east of defeated Mesopotamia—competed for control of Iraq. The area fell briefly under Persian control in 1508, but by 1534 the Ottoman Turks conquered much of it. Persian armies took control of Baghdad and large parts of Iraq in 1623. In 1638, Iraq again fell to the Ottomans. Iraq would remain under Turkish Ottoman control for almost three centuries.

This shift in power between Persians and Turks also deepened the conflict between the Sunni and Shia Arabs of Iraq. Persians were mostly Shia Muslims, and they favored the Iraqi Shias when Persians controlled the area. Turks, on the other hand, were Sunni Muslims, and during Ottoman control the Sunnis in Iraq were able to monopolize political power. This Sunni-Shia rift continues to play an important part in regional relations and politics in Iraq today.

MODERN HISTORY

Present-day Iraq occupies a territory much larger than Mesopotamia. The boundaries we know today were created from the fragments of the Turkish Ottoman Empire, after the Turks were defeated in World War I. European powers drew boundaries to geographically define the territories they inherited from the Turks. The territories of the Middle East had never before known fixed boundaries. They had always been parts of larger empires, and territory had always shifted between competing empires. Fixed boundaries were a very new concept.

The modern history of Iraq begins in the 1800s with the weakening of Ottoman rule and the rise of European influence in the Middle East.

Resistance to Ottoman Rule

During the period of Ottoman control, the province of Iraq was divided into three administrative districts: Mosul, Baghdad, and Basra. A series of local governors controlled the districts. They reported to and paid tribute to the Ottoman authorities. This relationship changed in 1869, when Midhat Pasha, a distinguished Ottoman official, was able to impose effective central control throughout the region. Pasha is credited with modernizing Baghdad in many ways, including transportation, the educational system, and basic needs such as sanitation. He also imposed his authority on the tribal countryside. For the first time, the Arabs felt the impact of a strong Ottoman government, especially with regard to tax collections.

In 1908, a new political group, the Young Turks, took power in Istanbul, the capital of Ottoman Turkey. The Young Turks instituted a "Turkification" policy throughout the Ottoman Empire that angered many Arabs, including those in Iraq. These changes included an emphasis on secular politics over Islamic law, and imposing Turkish culture, including language, in non-Turkish areas. The people of the Iraqi districts came to resent this direct foreign control, and this resentment gave rise to a strong sense of Arab nationalism and anti-Ottoman resistance.

Britain and Iraq

By the mid-1800s, European interest in the Ottoman territories had increased. As Ottoman control over their territories weakened, European powers pushed for commercial trade and competed for political influence in the region. By the end of the 1800s, Britain and Germany had become rivals in Mesopotamia.

The British were interested in Iraq as part of an overland route to India, and by 1861 they had established a steamship company for navigating the Tigris to the port of Basra. The route to India was critically important to Britain, because the British needed India's resources to fuel the vast British Empire. Germany had strong interest in the region as well, and announced plans to build a railroad from Berlin to Baghdad. British opposition to the project was ignored and the Ottoman government gave permission to the Germans to build a railroad from Baghdad to the Persian Gulf. The Germans continued to aid the Ottomans in other ways, and for the next several decades German influence in the Ottoman Empire continued to grow.

To overcome this move by the Germans, the British government strengthened its position in the Persian Gulf region by establishing treaties of protection with local Arab chieftains. In 1901, the British obtained permission to develop the oil fields of Iran.

When World War I began in 1914, the Turks chose to continue their ties with Germany. As an ally of Germany and Austria-Hungary, the Turks became the enemy of the British (and French), who opposed Germany during the war. In addition to the better-known campaigns in Europe, several battles during World War I were fought in the Ottoman Empire, as the British struggled to weaken this German ally and gain territory in the Middle East. Many of their efforts were aided by local Arab rulers and tribesmen who disliked the Ottomans and sought British cooperation to push the Turks out of Arab lands.

In 1914, a British army division landed at Al Faw in southern Iraq and occupied Basra. The landing filled the urgent British need to defend their oil interests in Iran. Steadily, the British Army advanced northward against strong Ottoman opposition and entered Baghdad in March 1917. The British and the Ottoman Turks signed a peace agreement in October 1918. Despite the treaty, the British army continued to advance north, capturing Mosul in early November. With this victory, Britain extended its rule over almost all of Iraq.

Elsewhere in the Ottoman Empire, Arab and British forces achieved great success in battles against the Turkish Army and were able to liberate much of Arabian territory. At the end of World War I (1918), the Ottoman government signed an armistice (an agreement ending a war) with the victorious British and French governments. These two European powers issued a joint statement about their plans to establish independent Arab states in the Arab regions that were formerly under control of the Ottoman Empire.

At the 1919 Paris Peace Conference, the victorious nations in World War I established the new territory of Iraq, encompassing the three former Ottoman districts of Mosul, Baghdad, and Basra. Because Britain was already occupying the Iraqi portion of former Ottoman lands, Iraq was given over to British control.

The Arabs felt betrayed by this turn of events and resented European control of their territories. Arab leaders had earlier been assured by the British that Arab territories liberated from Ottoman control would be given to the Arabs to control. When the Iraqi Arabs learned that the British were establishing boundaries for Iraq and administering the new state, they began an armed uprising against the British.

The British were forced to spend huge amounts of money to suppress the revolt, so they decided it would be best to withdraw from Mesopotamia. They quickly established a provisional government for the new state of Iraq, which would become a kingdom. Faisal, one of the Arab leaders who had aided the British during their battles with the Turks, was chosen as the ruler of the new state.

Britain wanted to attach the Kurdish lands to the new state of Iraq, because the British were well aware of the important oil resources around Kirkuk. Furthermore, the British-installed rulers of Iraq were mostly Sunni Arabs. Without the addition of the Sunni Kurds, the country would be overwhelmingly Shia. Adding Kurdish territory to Iraq increased the proportion of Sunni Muslims in the country. Sunni Arabs and Sunni Kurds together make up 40 percent of Iraq's population. Therefore, the northern Mosul district was drawn into the boundaries of the new Iraqi state.

In 1927, Faisal asked the British to support Iraq's application for admission to the League of Nations (an early version of the United Nations). A new treaty of alliance in 1930 included a recommendation by Britain that Iraq be admitted to the League of Nations as a free and independent state. In October 1932, Iraq joined the League of Nations as an independent sovereign (self-ruling) state. Faisal died in 1933 and was succeeded by his son Ghazi, a radical pan-Arab and anti-British figure.

Independent Iraq

In 1936, under King Ghazi, Iraq moved toward a pan-Arab alliance with the other nations of the Arab World. That year, the country experienced its first military *coup d'état* (overthrow) when the army overthrew the pan-Arab government. The coup opened the door to future military involvement in Iraqi politics. A moderate government was accepted by the king and held power until 1939. In April 1939, King Ghazi was killed in an automobile accident, leaving his three-year-old son, Faisal II, the titular (in title only) king. Between 1936 and 1941, there were seven attempts by different factions to seize power. The last attempt was sponsored by the Germans in April 1941, due

King Ghazi, pictured here shortly after taking the throne in 1933, salutes members of the Iraqi military as he descends the steps of the Parliament building in Baghdad. Ghazi was a staunch supporter of Pan-Arabism and opposed British involvement in Iraq's affairs.

in part to their displeasure with Iraq's alliance with the British (World War II was going on at this time and the Germans and British were enemies).

Adhering to a treaty of alliance with Britain, Iraq broke off diplomatic relations with Germany at the start of World War II (1939–1945). By 1942, Iraq had become a strategic supply center for British and U.S. forces operating in the Middle East and for the shipment of arms to the Union of Soviet Socialist Republics (USSR), then an ally of the United States and other forces aligned against Germany. In January 1943, Iraq declared war on Germany, the first independent Islamic state to do so. At the same time, Iraq's continued assistance to the Allied war effort enabled Arab leaders to make a stronger stand on behalf of a federation of Arab states. At the war's conclusion, the Arab League was formed when Iraq joined with other Arab nations in creating a regional association of sovereign states. In April 1947, the two kingdoms of Transjordan (present-day Jordan) and Iraq signed a treaty of kinship and alliance to provide for mutual military and diplomatic aid.

The first parliamentary elections based on direct voting took place in January 1953. These elections resulted in the founding of a pro-Western, pan-Arab government. King Faisal II formally assumed the throne on May 2, 1953, his eighteenth birthday. By this time, Iraq had made significant progress in its political, social, and economic development. This was due in part to the wise management of revenue received from the sale of its petroleum resources. There was a growing sense of nationalism in the young nation and a feeling that there should be less friendly relations with Western nations such as Britain. Iraq's leadership decided to follow Egypt's example: assert its independence and dedicate itself to the support of a pan-Arab state.

Republic of Iraq

In February 1958, Iraq and Jordan were united, following a conference between Faisal II and Hussein I, King of Jordan. The new union, which became known as the Arab Union of Jordan and Iraq, was established as a countermeasure to the United Arab Republic (UAR), a federation of Egypt and Syria formed in February of that year. The UAR bitterly opposed the pro-Western Arab Union and issued repeated radio calls urging the people, police, and army of Iraq to overthrow their government.

A sudden coup occurred on July 14, 1958, led by Iraqi general Abdul Karim Kassem, and the country was proclaimed a republic. King Faisal II, the crown prince, and Prime Minister Nuri al-Said were among those killed in the uprising. On July 15, the new government announced the establishment of close relations with the UAR and the disbanding of the Arab Union. General Kassem attempted to soothe and gain the confidence of the West by maintaining the flow of oil.

In June 1959, Iraq withdrew from the sterling bloc (a group of countries whose currencies were tied to the British pound sterling). A year later, the British protectorate over Kuwait ended, and Iraq claimed the area, asserting that Kuwait had been part of the Iraqi state at the time of its formation. To prevent an Iraqi invasion, British forces entered Kuwait in July 1960 at the invitation of the Kuwaiti ruler. The UN Security Council declined an Iraqi request to order the withdrawal of British troops.

The moves toward Pan-Arabism and away from the West alienated and angered the Kurds. This domestic unrest was briefly settled in early 1970, when the government agreed to form an autonomous (partially independent) Kurdish region, and Kurdish ministers were added to the cabinet. This created an uneasy peace between the Kurds and the Iraqi government.

In February 1963, General Kassem was overthrown and assassinated by a group of military officers, most of them members of the pan-Arab Baath Party. One of the active participants in the assassination of Kassem was Saddam Hussein, who had joined the Baath Party in 1959. His involvement with the killing of Kassem forced him to flee the country for several years. But he returned in 1963 and rose to a position of authority in the party. When the Baath Party rose to power through a coup in 1968, this high-ranking Baathist official began maneuvering for greater control of the party. In 1979, Saddam Hussein became Iraq's president and chairman of the Revolutionary Command Council.

The Hussein era was marked by a sense of national unity and internal security, but at the expense of civil liberties and regional autonomy. Opposition of any kind was brutally eliminated. Outspoken opponents, or those suspected of any crime, filled the many prisons of Iraq, or just "disappeared." The Kurdish opposition was ruthlessly suppressed by mass killings and chemical weapon attacks on Kurdish villages. Iraq's vast oil wealth was turned into a private treasure chest to enrich Hussein and his supporters. It was also used to torture and kill opponents and threaten and wage war on neighboring states.

Wars with Neighbors

Through the latter twentieth century, and especially after Saddam Hussein came to power in 1979, Iraq entered several decades of unrest and conflict with its neighbors. Massive oil revenues gave Iraq the ability to buy military equipment and support what eventually became the fifth-largest military force in the world. This power was—unfortunately for Iraq and its neighbors—guided by the Baathist Party's vision of a new pan-Arab empire, and controlled by a ruthless dictator with a quest for power. Saddam Hussein saw himself as a modern-day Nebuchadnezzar II. He believed himself to be a great Mesopotamian leader who would unite the Arab World under his Baathist government and bring the Arab nation back into a Golden Age.

Iran-Iraq War (1980–1988)

In 1979, Islamic revolutionaries in Iran overthrew the country's secular (non-Islamic) government and established an Islamic republic. Tension between the Iraqi government and Iran's new Islamic regime increased during that year when unrest among Iranian Kurds spilled over into Iraq. Growing hostility between Sunni and Shia religious groups, in both Iran and Iraq, created further tension.

In 1980, war broke out between Iran and Iraq following a long period of dispute focusing particularly upon control of the Shatt al-Arab. Basra, Iraq's main port city, lies along this waterway, which carries the Tigris and Euphrates flow into the Persian Gulf. This region also contains Iran's port city of Khorramshahr and the Abadan oil refineries.

In September 1980, Iraq invaded Iran over the disputed Shatt al-Arab, the waterway that flows into the Persian Gulf. During the first months of the war, the Iraqi Army invaded the Iranian port city of Khorramshahr, which is pictured here shortly after being laid to waste by Iraqi forces.

The 1975 Algiers Agreement between Iran and Iraq granted the oil-rich borderlands along the Shatt al-Arab to Iran, in exchange for Iranian promises to stop supporting Kurdish rebels in Iraq. By 1979, Saddam Hussein had come to power in Iraq. He broke the Algiers Agreement and tried to shift the disputed border back to Iraq. He used the excuse that the mostly Arab population of Iran's border region would prefer being part of the predominantly Arab state of Iraq.

Iraq stirred up Arab nationalism by encouraging Iran's Arabs in the border region to rise against the Persian government of Iran. Shia-controlled Iran stirred up religious differences by urging the majority Shia Muslims in southern Iraq to shake off their Sunni rulers. After initial border clashes, Iraq started the war. Iraq believed that Iran could offer little resistance, because they were internationally isolated after the fundamentalist revolution removed the Shah of Iran (the shah was very pro-West and a friend of many Western governments). Also, Iran's internal affairs were in chaos and its army demoralized after the ousting of the shah (king).

Iraqi forces seized large areas of the Iran-Iraq frontier but captured no large cities. Iran declared a holy war and set upon Iraq with a vengeance, taking back all that Iraq had gained plus taking the Iraqi Shatt al-Arab (and Iraq's only ports). Iraq then sued for peace but Iran was not ready to halt the fight. Nothing more was gained by either country. Both sides fought an eight-year war of attrition (trying to outlast their enemy), with many fierce battles and long periods of stalemate. Both sides agreed to a cease-fire in 1988. The war was never ended by an agreement, but the cease-fire ended hostilities.

Gulf War I (1991)

When Iraq invaded Iran in 1980, the West was not too concerned about Iraq. The United States even developed a clear "tilt" toward Iraq and gave both secret and visible aid to Saddam's war against Iran.

Iraq's 1990 invasion of Kuwait was a different matter. Iraq was branded a "pariah nation" and its leader (Saddam) a "new Hitler." The scene was set for a brief but devastating war, with thousands of (mostly) Iraqi casualties and extensive environmental damage.

In 1990, Iraq renewed its long-standing claim to the territory of Kuwait. Although Kuwait had helped Iraq during its war with Iran, Iraq claimed that overproduction of petroleum by Kuwait was injuring Iraq's economy by lowering the price of crude oil. Iraq also claimed that Kuwaitis were drilling into Iraqi oil fields using horizontal wells, extending underground from the Kuwaiti side of the border. Iraqi troops invaded Kuwait on August 2 and rapidly took over the country. The UN Security Council issued a series of resolutions that condemned the occupation, imposed broad trade restrictions on Iraq, and demanded that Iraq withdraw from Kuwait by January 15, 1991. Iraq did not comply with the demands of the United Nations. A coalition (allied group) of nations led by the United States began an intense bombing campaign that targeted military sites and strategic resources in Iraq and occupied Kuwait in January 1991.

The Persian Gulf War proved to be an international embarrassment for Iraq, which was forced out of Kuwait in about six weeks. Coalition forces invaded southern Iraq, and tens of thousands of Iraqis were killed. Many of the country's armored vehicles and artillery pieces were destroyed, and its nuclear and chemical weapons facilities were severely damaged.

In April 1991, Iraq agreed to UN terms for a permanent cease-fire. Coalition troops withdrew from southern Iraq as a UN peacekeeping force moved in to police the Iraq-Kuwait border. Meanwhile, Hussein used his remaining military forces to crush rebellions by Shias in the south and Kurds in the north. Hundreds of thousands of Kurdish refugees fled to Turkey and Iran. Ultimately, U.S., British, and French troops moved inside Iraq's northern border to protect the Kurds from Iraqi government reprisals. International forces set up "no-fly zones" in both northern and southern Iraq to keep Iraqi air forces out of these areas to improve the safety of the Kurdish and Shia populations.

In 1994, Saddam Hussein signed a decree accepting Kuwait's political independence. The agreement ended Iraq's claim to Kuwait as a province of Iraq.

In order to end the invasion of its territory, the Iraqi government had agreed to destroy its chemical and biological weapons, terminate nuclear weapons programs, and accept international inspections to ensure that these conditions were met. Iraq later claimed that its withdrawal from Kuwait was enough and ignored its other promises. This breach of promises led to trade restrictions against Iraq. Equipment and basic supplies were prohibited from being shipped by any country to Iraq.

Gulf War II (2003)

Because of the trade sanctions, Iraq faced a serious economic crisis by 1995. Prices were high and shortages of food and medicine were common. The Iraqi dinar (monetary unit) was worthless outside of Iraq. To reduce the humanitarian impact of sanctions, the UN Security Council voted in April 1995 to allow Iraq to sell limited amounts of oil to meet its urgent human needs (food and medicine). In 1998, the UN increased the amount of oil that Iraq was allowed to sell. Iraq was unable to take full advantage of this increase, because the lack of imported equipment had reduced its production capabilities.

In December 1998, Iraq declared that it would no longer comply with UN inspection teams. It called for an end to the sanctions and threatened to fire on aircraft patrolling the "no-fly zones." Until the outbreak of war in 2003, Iraq continued to challenge the patrols while, in retaliation, British and U.S. planes struck Iraqi missile launch sites and other targets. Iraq was also said to be associated with the terror movement that led to the September 11, 2001 terrorist attacks in the United States, though the connection was never proved.

The 2003 Gulf War II involved a U.S. and British invasion of Iraq to remove Saddam Hussein from power and to locate presumed "weapons of mass destruction" (which were never found). With Saddam Hussein gone, U.S. and British forces set about the business of government change and nation building as part of a broader sociopolitical agenda (that is, democracy in Iraq was to be used as a catalyst for broad change and reform in the Middle East).

These moves have been countered by a small but effective resistance from both foreign and Iraqi insurgents that continued through 2006. The foreign fighters are mostly religious

Shortly after U.S.–led coalition forces deposed Saddam Hussein on April 9, 2003, many Iraqis joined together in denouncing the U.S. occupation of Iraq. Here, Sunni and Shia Muslims demonstrate near Baghdad's Abu-Hanifa Mosque on April 18, 2003.

extremists opposed to non-Muslim (U.S. and British) invasion of a Muslim country. Some Iraqi insurgents are Sunni Arabs loyal to Saddam Hussein. Others are just angry at the loss of Sunni control and the corresponding rise of Shia and Kurdish influence in the country.

4

People and Culture

Most of Iraq's people speak the same language and practice the same religion. This apparent uniformity of culture and faith hides the many differences that exist in the country. Where these identities become entrenched as regional differences—as between the Sunni and Shia Arabs, or as Kurds versus Arabs—relations may be complicated. Peoples' actions are shaped by their worldviews, which are based on their identities, which in turn are shaped by language, religion, and ethnic affiliation. Understanding the patterns of population, language, and religion across Iraq will help to make sense of historic and political changes in the country.

POPULATION AND SETTLEMENT

The early population of Mesopotamia was relatively large, especially compared to areas in North America or Europe in ancient times. A densely settled Mesopotamian population made possible the development of advanced, socially complex societies in ancient Iraq. However, the population growth rate was never very high. Until the mid-1900s, Iraqi society had little control over fertility (average births per female) or mortality (death rates). Increases in the population over the past century have resulted mainly from a reduced death rate.

Many families in Iraq live in rural areas, where large numbers of children are preferred, because they can help with farming, herding, and other chores. The average family size in cities is smaller, but still tends to be larger than urban families in the United States. The Islamic tradition encourages large families and often discourages birth control. Marriage commonly takes place at an early age and child bearing begins soon after marriage. Because of these traditions, birthrates remain high, even after new medical and sanitation technologies have reduced death rates. The combination of high birthrates and a lowered death rate have been responsible for the rapid growth of Iraq's population since the 1950s. Iraq's population growth rate is now about 2.7 percent (1,027 births for every 1,000 deaths). At this high rate of growth, the Iraqi population will double in about 26 years.

Iraq's population density is 154 persons per square mile (59 per square kilometer). This figure is somewhat misleading, however, because the actual density varies greatly across the country. Small numbers of people live in western Iraq; some in dusty villages and some as *Bedouin* nomads (people who move their tent dwellings as they follow domestic herds of sheep, goats, and camels). A minority population of Kurds lives in small mountain villages in the mountains of northeast Iraq, or in the cities in the foothills. Most people in Iraq live in towns and villages along the Jazirah Plateau and Mesopotamian Plain, from the Turkish border to the Persian Gulf. About 70 percent of the population resides in urban areas.

Iraq's population of about 27 million is approximately 75 percent Arab, 20 percent Kurdish, and includes a small percentage of minorities such as ethnic Turkomans, Assyrians,

Armenians, Persians, and Jews. Iraqis tend to feel a common national sentiment, and most of them share a common language and religion, in spite of differing racial origins. Given the long history of Iraq, this racial diversity is not surprising. Iraq has experienced many conquests and occupations by different peoples and cultures.

ETHNICITY AND LANGUAGE

Because the mixing of races is widespread in the Middle East, an attempt to group people according to race (physical characteristics) would be difficult and inexact. The ethnic groups of Iraq are more commonly classified by the languages they speak. Iraqis speak 23 different native languages, though Arabic dominates the group.

Arabs

Arabs are a racially mixed people whose primary language is Arabic. The physical appearance of Arabs varies considerably. They are linked through a common history, a common language, and the sharing of common social customs and manners. About 75 percent of Iraq's population is Arab. Most of Iraq's Arabs are Shia Muslim, many are Sunni Muslim, and a few are Christian Arab.

Arabic is a Semitic language (along with Hebrew, the Jewish language). The Akkadians, among the earliest inhabitants of ancient Mesopotamia, were Semitic tribes, so Arab cousins have been part of the cultural mix of Iraq for a very long time.

Until the revelations of Muhammad and the spread of the Islamic faith, classical Arabic was spoken only by nomads and sparsely settled groups in the Arabian Peninsula. Along with the rise of Islam (seventh century), Arabic spread rapidly. It soon replaced existing languages in Iraq and elsewhere in the Middle East and North Africa. In Iraq, Semitic Akkadian (related to Arabic) had been spoken for thousands of years. But Akkadian, along with Assyrian, Persian, and other languages, was replaced by Arabic as the dominant language of the region. Almost all Iraqis today—even the Kurds, Turkomen, and other minorities—speak some Arabic.

Throughout most of Iraq, the Mesopotamian dialect (variety) is the principal variety of spoken Arabic. In the western desert of Iraq, the Najdi dialect of Arabic is more common, especially among the Bedouin communities. In the southeast around Basra, Gulf Arabic is spoken by a small number of Iraqis.

Kurds

The Kurds (from the Persian word *gurd*, or hero) inhabit an isolated, mountainous frontier, where they have lived for more than 3,000 years. Ever since European powers carved up the Ottoman Empire to create the boundaries of new Middle Eastern countries, the Kurds have been trying to get their own Kurdish state—Kurdistan—with their own boundaries to surround Kurdish territory. The Kurds remain the largest ethnic group in the world not represented by their own country. They speak their own language—Kurdish, a form of Persian— and have a keen sense of their own heritage.

The Kurds maintain loyalty to their own tribal organizations. Loyalty to tribe, rather than state, has placed them in conflict with the governments of countries they inhabit. For centuries, the Kurds have subsisted—and many still do—by raising sheep and goats in the hills and valleys of Iraq's mountains. Traditionally, Kurds are proud, warlike, and fiercely independent.

More Kurds live in Turkey than in any other country (as many as 12 million). As many as 7 million live in Iran and about 5 million in Iraq. Smaller numbers live in Syria, Armenia, and Azerbaijan. Because their homeland is split among several countries, Kurds are a minority group in every country they inhabit. They make up about 20 percent of the population of Iraq.

Although they are a minority in Iraq, Kurds are the majority population in the country's northern mountains. Iraqi

Kurds, who are the largest ethnic group in the world not represented by their own country, are predominately Sunni Muslim. They make up approximately 20 percent of Iraq's population and largely reside in the northeastern part of the country. Pictured here is a group of Kurdish women participating in a traditional dance during a wedding party in Sulaymaniyah.

Kurds have long demanded self-government in Kurdistan, the use of Kurdish language in schools, and a greater share of the country's oil revenues.

The 1970 constitution named Arabs and Kurds as the two nationalities of the Iraqi nation and (on paper) established Kurdish autonomy. After Saddam Hussein came to power in 1979, Iraq launched military operations against the Kurds, which continued off and on through the 1980s. At the end of the war with Iran in 1988, the Iraqi army turned on the Kurds in a savage campaign of genocide. "Operation Anfal" launched chemical attacks on Kurdish villages and forcibly deported Kurdish villagers.

After Gulf War I (1991), Kurdish rebels in the north were brutally suppressed by the Iraqi Army and many Kurds fled as refugees into neighboring Kurdish areas of Turkey. The United States and its allies sent troops to the Iraq-Turkey border and created a "no-fly zone," barring Iraqi aircraft north of the 36th parallel—north of Kirkuk—the main Kurdish area. This buffered Iraq's Kurdish population from direct control by Iraq's government.

Under protection of the "no-fly zone" and with U.S. troops in the region, Iraq's Kurdish population seized the opportunity to organize themselves. They organized their militia (the *peshmerga*) and created a two-party system of government. As a result, the Iraqi Kurds—unlike Kurds in surrounding countries—are well organized, politically democratic, and protected by their own forces.

Since Gulf War II (2003), the Kurdish people have been walking a fine line between openly breaking from Iraq and maneuvering for greater autonomy (self-government) within a federal Iraq. The new system of government in Iraq does not give the Kurds an independent state but does grant them much autonomy. Iraq's Kurds now refer to their territory as "Kurdistan." Maps of Kurdistan showing all the Kurdish lands are sold in shops, and the flag of Kurdistan flies in public places. Kurdish cities are referred to by their Kurdish names, not their Arabic names (where there is a difference), and these names are printed on maps, city signs, and airports. This open display of Kurdish nationalism would not be allowed in Kurdish Iran, Syria, or Turkey. The Iraqi Kurds have come closest to realizing their dream of a Kurdistan.

Other Ethnic Minorities

Although Kurds are the largest ethnic minority in Iraq, other minorities also live in certain areas of Iraq. Turkomen make up 2 percent of the Iraqi population. They live in villages in the northeast and in the cities of Kirkuk, Mosul, and Arbil in the foothill zone. Racially, the Turkomen are descendants of Mongol invaders from Central Asia who were led by the conquerer Tamerlane in their conquest of Iraq nearly 700 years ago. Most Turkomen are Sunni Muslims.

Also in the Kurdish mountains of northern Iraq, the Assyrians are descendants of ancient Mesopotamian people who speak Aramaic (Syriac). They are Iraq's third-largest ethnic minority group but make up less than 1 percent of the population. They are mostly Christian in faith, following the Christian Nestorian, Chaldean, Jacobite, Syrian Orthodox, or Syrian Catholic Church. They have integrated well into Iraqi society.

Also widely accepted as equal members of society are the Armenians—Christian refugees pushed out of eastern Turkey by the Ottoman Turks. A large Armenian population lives in Baghdad, where they maintain their own language, religion, and trading community.

A small number of people of Persian (Iranian) descent settled in and around the Shia holy cities of Najaf, Karbala, Samarra, and Kadhimain. During the war with Iran, many fled back to Iran.

Jews have lived in Iraq for more than 2,500 years. In the mid-twentieth century, at least 130,000 Jews resided there. They generally lived in urban areas, often working as merchants, professionals, and government officials in Baghdad. More than 120,000 have moved to Israel since the Jewish state was created in 1948, and several thousand have gone to Iran. Small numbers of Iraqi Jews remain in the country, mostly in the north and in Baghdad.

The Bedouin are not an ethnic or religious group, though most speak Arabic and practice the Islamic faith. The Bedouin are nomadic tribes who migrate seasonally between western and southern Iraq, and between the neighboring countries of Kuwait and Saudi Arabia. Winters are often spent in southern areas, where vegetation is abundant; whereas summers are spent near the oases on the edge of Iraq's western desert. The Bedouin raise domesticated livestock and obtain most of their food, clothing, and shelter from their herds of sheep, goats, and camels. The Bedouin live a modest and harsh life. Many have abandoned their traditional existence for village life. As a result, the number of Bedouin who live as nomads has declined, although they remain a common sight in the western desert of Iraq.

RELIGION

To understand Iraq's cultural diversity and group relations, it helps to perceive religion as more than a collection of theological beliefs and places of worship. Religion, like language and ethnic affiliation, is an important part of individual identity and group relations. Religion has the power to move people to accomplish great deeds of kindness, or contributes to unrest where competing religious ideologies are rooted in the same place. Religion also influences dietary practices, agricultural practices, workweek schedules, legal codes, ethical norms of conduct, and other elements of culture.

Islam: Sunni and Shia

Islam (seventh century) is a relatively recent arrival to Iraq, compared to Christianity (first century) or Judaism (about 2000 B.C.). All three are monotheistic faiths (belief in one God), and all three worship the God of Abraham. Muslims (followers of Islam) make up almost 97 percent of Iraq's population. Like all major faiths, Islam has its sectarian divisions—Sunni and Shia (like Orthodox, Catholic, and Protestant divisions within Christianity). The Shias are found primarily in central and southern Iraq, and the Sunnis mostly reside in the center and north of the country. Iraqi Arabs may be Sunni or Shia; most Kurds are Sunni.

About 60 to 65 percent of Iraqi Muslims follow the Shia branch of Islam and the rest follow the Sunni branch. Sunnis are the minority sect in Iraq, but are the majority in world Islam. About 83 percent of Muslims worldwide follow Sunni Islam.

Although the majority of Iraq's Muslims are Shias, Sunni Muslims have ruled the nation since the seventh century. The rift between the two sects was accentuated during Saddam Hussein's reign, when the Sunni leader openly persecuted Shias. Despite the animosity between the two denominations, approximately 2 million of Iraq's 6.5 million married couples, including this husband and wife, are Sunni-Shia unions.

Sunnis also control the governments of most Islamic nations, as they did in Iraq until the overthrow of Saddam Hussein.

Sunni Muslims believe that the prophet Muhammad died in 632 without designating a successor. Elders of the religious community would select a caliph (Arabic: *khalifah*) as political leader of the Islamic community-state. Sunni Islam gives religious authority to the *ulema* (religious scholars) who offer collective judgment to guide the community of believers (*ummah*: Islamic nation).

Shia Muslims believe that Muhammad—on his deathbed—designated his son-in-law (and cousin), Ali, to lead the community. They maintain that the *Imam* (leader) of the Muslim community must be descended from the Prophet's family, through the bloodline of the prophet and Ali. The Imam is both the religious and political leader of the community. When the fourth and last "Righteous Caliph" (Ali) was murdered in 661, he was canonized as "Saint Ali" and his followers—the Shias—split from orthodox Sunni Islam.

The word *Islam* means "submission to the will of God" (or Allah in Arabic). The faith of Islam is summed up in the *Shahada*, or profession of faith: "There is no God but God, and Muhammad is his prophet." Saying the Shahada once, aloud, with understanding and belief is necessary to become a Muslim. This profession of faith is the first of the Five Pillars of Islam. The other four pillars are: *Salaht*, or prescribed prayer; *Zakat*, or charitable giving to the poor and needy; *Ramadan*, fasting from dawn to dusk during the ninth month of the Muslim calendar; and the *Hajj*, or pilgrimage to Mecca, in Saudi Arabia.

The Koran (*Qur'an*) is the holy book that contains the inspired words of Muhammad given by God through the Angel Gabriel. Muslims honor this book and believe it contains what they need for salvation. Also, Muslims believe that the Christian gospels, the first five books of the Old Testament, and the Psalms are the inspired words of God, passed down through prophets who came before Muhammad. Muslims do recognize Adam, Noah, Abraham, Moses, and Jesus as great prophets, but for them Muhammad is the true, last, and greatest prophet.

Muslims are required to pray five times a day while facing Mecca, the birthplace and most holy site of Islam. A public place of prayer and worship is called a mosque, which functions in the same way as a church for Christians. From *minarets* (towers) of the mosque, the *muezzin* (person who makes the call for prayer) will call the faithful to prayer at the required times. In times past, the muezzin would climb the tower stairs to call for prayer. In modern times, the call is made into a microphone and broadcast from speakers mounted high on the minarets. Friday is the day when Muslims gather in large numbers at their mosques to pray and hear a sermon (like Sunday for Christians). The preachers, also called imams, are teachers, not priests. Islam does not have a formal priesthood with religious authority to stand between the worshiper and God.

Giving to the poor and the mosques is also a requirement. Even though a Zakat authority (state-provided welfare system) has replaced some individual giving, generosity to others is highly valued.

Fasting is required during the holy month of Ramadan, the ninth month in the Islamic calendar. No food, drink, tobacco, or other worldly pleasure may be consumed from dawn until sunset. This is done to symbolically reenact the Prophet's fast, which preceded his revelation from God. Exceptions are made for the sick, the weak, soldiers, and travelers. Ramadan falls at different times in different years (relative to the calendar with which most Westerners are familiar), because it is determined by a calendar based on the moon.

Pilgrimage to Mecca, at least once in a lifetime, is expected of every Muslim who is physically or financially able to go. Only Muslims are allowed in the holy cities of Mecca and Medina in Saudi Arabia. Pilgrims who make the journey earn an elevated status in their community upon their return.

As with other religions, adherence to these practices varies. For example, not all Muslims respond to each prayer call, though most of the faithful will at the very least attend Friday prayers.

OTHER RELIGIONS

Christians are Iraq's largest religious minority, making up about 3 percent of the country's population. They are descendants of people who did not convert to Islam during the Arab conquest of the seventh and eighth centuries. Christianity predates Islam, and Christians have had a strong presence in the country since early in the Christian era.

One of the earliest and largest Christian groups is the Nestorian Assyrians, with more than 500,000 members scattered from the Syrian border, to Arbil, Kirkuk, and Baghdad in Iraq. A related group, the Chaldeans, is centered in Mosul and Baghdad. These Arabic-speaking Iraqis are the largest Christian group in the country. The Chaldeans are related to ancient Semitic people who once ruled Babylonia.

The Sabeans (also called Subba or Mandaeans) are another Christian minority found in Iraq. They are sometimes called the Christians of Saint John, because they claim to be followers of John the Baptist (a revered prophet to both Muslims and Christians). Their beliefs are closely tied to the Islamic faith. Originally dwelling near the riverbanks in southern Iraq, they are master boatbuilders. This is not surprising, because their religion requires that they live next to running water.

In northwest Iraq, near Jebel Sinjar, live the Yazidis (from the Persian *Yazdan,* meaning God). The Yazidis are ethnically Kurdish and speak a Kurdish dialect but use Arabic in their worship. They have a unique religion that fuses Zoroastrian, Manichean, Christian, Jewish, and pagan elements with Islam. They regard both the Koran and the Bible as holy books.

Small communities of Jews call Iraq home. These people trace their ancestry back to the Babylonian exile of the Jewish people that occurred from 586 to 516 B.C. As previously mentioned, Iraqi Jews have declined in number in recent years.

5

Government and Politics

For most of its history, the territory that is now Iraq has known only a monarchy system of government (king, shah, sultan, or emperor). Even after the Ottoman sultan was removed, a new king (Faisal) was installed by the British. Beginning with the coup of 1958 that brought General Kassem to power, Iraq was proclaimed a republic and ruled by a series of military strongmen. The last in this line was Saddam Hussein. All contributed to the modernization and development of the country, but they also contributed to themselves. Misuse of the national income and corruption in government are problems common to many developing countries. But nowhere did these problems more completely drain the national treasury and national potential than in Saddam Hussein's Iraq.

GOVERNMENT AFTER INDEPENDENCE

In October 1932, Iraq joined the League of Nations as an independent, sovereign (self-ruling) state. At that time, it was still a monarchy (ruled by a king). Military officers overthrew the monarchy in a bloody coup d'état and set up a republic in 1958. Since 1968, the government has been a dictatorship dominated by a single political party, the Baath Party (the party officially recognized). The Iraqi people have had little or no say in their government.

The Baath Party ruled Iraq through a nine-member Revolutionary Command Council (RCC), which enacted legislation by formal decree. The RCC's president, who also served as the chief of state and supreme commander of the armed forces, was elected by a two-thirds majority of the RCC. The president appointed all government, civil service, and military personnel and approved the budget. The RCC named Saddam Hussein president in 1979. There were no constitutional provisions limiting the terms of office of the president, so in 1990, he was named "President for Life." He remained in the position until he was overthrown by the U.S.–led invasion of 2003.

Iraq had no national legislature until 1980, when a National Assembly was established. This assembly consisted of 250 members, 220 of whom were elected by popular vote and 30 who were appointed by the president to represent the three northern provinces. A candidate for the National Assembly had to demonstrate "loyalty to the principles of the Baath Revolution." The task of the National Assembly was to approve or reject legislation proposed by the RCC. With few exceptions, however, the National Assembly merely "rubber-stamped" (automatically passed) every RCC action.

Until 2003, Iraq was governed under a provisional (temporary) constitution that was enacted in 1970 and amended through the years. This constitution defined Iraq as "a sovereign people's democratic republic," dedicated to Pan-Arabism—the ultimate realization of a single Arab state—and

In April 2003, U.S.–led coalition forces overthrew Iraqi president Saddam Hussein and established an interim government known as the Coalition Provisional Authority (CPA). After Hussein was deposed, many Iraqis rejoiced by toppling statues of Hussein throughout the country, including this one in the northern town of Kirkuk.

to the establishment of a socialist system. The document declared Islam as the state religion but guaranteed freedom of religion. It defined the Iraqi people as being composed of two principal nationalities, Arab and Kurdish. A 1974 amendment granted autonomy for the Kurds in areas where they constitute a majority, but stated that Iraq was to remain united and undivided. The state was given the important central role in "planning, directing, and guiding" the economy, and national resources were defined as "the property of the people."

From 1968 to 1978, under President Ahmed Hassan al-Bakr, the Baath Party ruled the country with an iron fist. Within the party, however, top-level discussions were conducted in a fairly free fashion. Decisions were often made through a discussion of party leaders, after taking an internal vote. In 1979, this semidemocracy ended after Saddam Hussein came to power, replacing al-Bakr as president.

Immediately, Hussein had 55 senior party members and army officers executed for treason, even though there was no real evidence of betrayal. The most likely reason for their elimination was either opposition to Hussein's replacing al-Bakr, or a dispute over the way in which Hussein was elected. Throughout Hussein's rule, there were many such executions for "disloyalty," sending an unmistakable message that no one was to question his decisions.

After Hussein rose to power, there were occasional legislative elections. These "elections" gave the false impression that democratic rule was firmly established, but these elections were nothing more than a front. The people did not really elect their rulers, because only candidates authorized by the Baath Party could stand for election. The Iraqi regime would not tolerate any form of resistance. Therefore, opposition parties either operated illegally as exiles from neighboring countries, or in areas of northern Iraq outside the regime's control.

Iraq is a charter member of the United Nations and a founding member of the Arab League, which organizes peacekeeping forces among its members and engages in social and cultural activities. Iraq is also a founding member of the Organization of Petroleum Exporting Countries (OPEC), and the Organization of the Islamic Conference, which promotes solidarity among nations where Islam is an important religion.

PROVINCIAL GOVERNMENT

The Baathist government that was removed in 2003 maintained strong centralized authority over Iraq. The government in Baghdad controlled Iraq's 18 separate provinces by appointing a governor to oversee each political region. Councils headed by mayors ran the cities and towns. As a concession to the Kurds in the 1970 constitution, three of the provinces were designated a Kurdish autonomous (semi-independent) region and had less central government control over their affairs. The Kurdish autonomous region had an elected 50-member legislature. This region came under United Nations and coalition (U.S. and allies) protection after the first Gulf War, to prevent Hussein from taking military action against rebellious Kurds.

Government functions since the second Gulf War (2003) have continued to administer Iraq through the 18 provinces. Recent elections of government officials, and votes on whether to accept the new constitution, have all been administered at the provincial level. The new Iraqi constitution of 2005 incorporates a federal system of government, which gives more local control to each of the provinces (much like U.S. states with their own governments). The provinces now send elected officials to represent them in the central government, which itself was newly elected in late 2005.

GOVERNMENT IN TRANSITION

The government of Iraq has been in transition since the U.S. occupation began in March 2003. As U.S. forces moved into Baghdad in March of that year, the Baathist government led by Saddam Hussein fled the capital or went into hiding. Many fled the country. The U.S. established an interim (temporary) government in Baghdad, called the Coalition Provisional Authority (CPA), with U.S. administrator Paul Bremer serving as head of government. During this period of U.S. control, the Baath Party—formerly the only legal political party in Iraq—was disbanded.

A new Iraqi government to replace the Baathists was created in several steps during 2003–2005. First, the interim government under Paul Bremer appointed a 25-member Governing Council to begin the job of creating an interim constitution. To make the process more democratic, the Governing

Council was made up of representatives from a wide cross section of Iraqi society, including women, Sunni Arabs, Shia Arabs, Kurds, Turkomen, and Assyrian Christians. There were many debates at this time among council members, and among ordinary Iraqis and the international media, over the style of government that the new Iraq should adopt. Some groups wanted a strong central government. Others wanted a federal state, with more power given to the provinces. Some wanted an Islamic regime, or a government guided by *sharia* (Islamic law). Others wanted a clear separation of church and state and pushed for a secular (nonreligious) form of government.

In March 2004, the members of this council endorsed an interim constitution to create a federal-style Iraq. The legal system underpinning the constitution was based on a combination of civil (secular) and Islamic law. The constitution included a 13-article Bill of Rights, and served as the basis for electing a National Assembly to replace the Governing Council. In June 2004, the U.S.–administered Coalition Provisional Authority transferred control of the government to the Iraqi Interim Government (IIG). However, the United States and Great Britain kept military forces in the country to help the new Iraqi police and army maintain internal security.

Democratic elections were held in January 2005 for a Transitional National Assembly (TNA). These were the first real democratic elections in Iraq's history. The TNA had responsibility for drafting the permanent Iraqi Constitution, much like the Continental Congress was responsible for drafting the U.S. Constitution in 1787. The new constitution, completed in August 2005, incorporated the principles of democracy and a federal system for Iraq. In a federal system, the governments in each province (or state) are elected locally and send representatives to the National Assembly. This system allows the different groups in Iraq—Sunnis, Shias, and Kurds—to maintain regional control over their territory and allows the regions to decide how much power to give to the central government.

On December 15, 2005, Iraqi citizens went to the polls to cast ballots in the nation's first parliamentary election. Here, constituents, who are backdropped by campaign posters, wait in line to vote in the central Iraq town of Samarra.

This new federal constitution has been strongly supported by the Shia and Kurdish population of Iraq—the groups historically dominated by the minority Sunni Arab population. However, most Sunnis have not been happy with the situation. Some of them have led a campaign of violence, using car bombs and assassinations to try to disrupt the political process.

A nationwide referendum was held in October 2005 to see if the people of Iraq would support the new constitution. The referendum passed, with majority support for the new constitution.

However, not everyone was happy with the outcome. Provinces with a majority Shia population (central and south Iraq) and majority Kurdish population (in the north) overwhelmingly supported the new constitution. Sunni provinces (central and western Iraq) showed either very narrow support or voted against it. The main Sunni concern was that the federal system endorsed by the constitution gives too much local power to the provinces, leaving the central government weak. The central government is the platform that minority Sunni leaders have used to control and dominate Iraq for centuries. Federal authority in the provinces gives more power to the majority Shia population, and gives a minority Kurdish population some control in the central government for the first time.

Passage of the Iraqi Constitution paved the way for the last step in Iraq's political transformation: a federal government, constitutionally established through national elections in December 2005. As this book goes to press in late 2006, Iraq's political future remains uncertain. Terrorist acts continue on almost a daily basis and some observers believe that the country is on the brink of civil war. Only time (and patience) will determine whether Iraq will be able to achieve political stability, which is so essential if the country and its people are to enjoy peace and prosperity.

CHAPTER

6

Iraq's Economy

Money and jobs are needed if a country is to prosper and its people enjoy a good life. The economy refers to how a country earns income and how its people make a living. Like its government, Iraq's economy is in transition. Oil is still the most important commodity, and many industries continue to operate that have provided jobs for decades. But years of economic sanctions have finally come to an end and Iraq is now receiving supplies and new technologies that were prohibited by trade restrictions for more than a dozen years. The Iraqi economy has opened up to the world and Iraq is primed for rapid economic growth.

OIL AND OTHER NATURAL RESOURCES

Iraq has abundant oil resources and its economy is dominated by the oil sector (area of the economy). For many decades, oil has provided more than 90 percent of Iraq's foreign exchange earnings (money earned in international markets). In the Middle East, Iraq has the largest oil reserves after Saudi Arabia and Iran, theoretically making it one of the richest countries in the world. However, because of war, corruption, poor management, and the economic sanctions forced on Iraq after it invaded Kuwait, Iraq's economy was severely damaged. Iraqis became the region's poorest people. This economic decline can be reversed, because Iraq is still one of the leading oil producers in the world. Profits from oil sales can be invested to improve other sectors of the economy, such as manufacturing and agriculture.

Oil

Iraq's proven oil reserves—115 billion barrels—is fourth largest in the world and amounts to an estimated 10 percent of the world's supply. The largest oil fields are located in two main regions: in the southeast around Basra, inland from the Persian Gulf, and in the northern part of the country, in the plains and foothills around Kirkuk. The country is believed to have deeper oil deposits in the western desert region, though oil in this area has not yet been explored. Iraq also has large reserves of natural gas. Most of this gas is found in association with oil, so as more oil is produced, more natural gas is extracted.

In the early twentieth century, Iraq's population was highly rural and its economy was mostly agricultural. Oil was discovered and tapped in the 1920s and the country soon became economically dependent on the oil industry.

By 1972, the government had nationalized the Iraq Petroleum Company (IPC), which had been owned by foreign oil companies. In 1973, Iraq also worked as a member of the Organization of Petroleum Exporting Countries (OPEC) to engineer a steep rise in the price of crude oil. The nationalization of Iraqi oil, combined with the increase in the price of oil, had the effect of raising Iraq's oil revenues more than eightfold—from $1 billion in 1972 to $8.2 billion in 1975.

The region around the northern city of Kirkuk is home to one of Iraq's two major oil reserves. Pictured here is an Iraqi oil worker at the country's oldest oil processing plant near the Baba Gurgur oil field, outside of Kirkuk. Founded in 1927, Baba Gurgur was once the largest oil field in the world until the Gawar oil field was discovered in Saudi Arabia in the 1950s.

Before the outbreak of the war with Iran in September 1980, Iraq's economic prospects were bright. Oil production had reached a level of 3.5 million barrels per day, and oil revenues were $21 billion in 1979 and $27 billion in 1980. Just before the fighting began, Iraq had collected an estimated $35 billion in foreign exchange reserves.

The effects of the war with Iran were ruinous. Iraq's foreign exchange reserves were depleted, its economy crumbled, and the country was burdened with a foreign debt of more than $40 billion. At the war's end, oil exports gradually increased with the construction of new pipelines and the repair of damaged facilities. But Iraq's invasion of Kuwait in 1990, the trade restrictions that followed, and damage from military action by an international military alliance in 1991 drastically reduced economic activity.

From 1996 until Gulf War II in 2003, the United Nations allowed Iraq to trade some of its oil every year to buy essential supplies such as food and medicine for the country. This "oil-for-food program" provided some relief from the sanctions and improved conditions for the average Iraqi citizen. However, this program could not solve the fundamental problems of a devastated economy, a population impoverished by three wars in three decades, many years of severe economic sanctions, and a corrupt government.

Since the end of Gulf War II, American investments in Iraq's oil infrastructure have again increased output. Oil now accounts for almost 90 percent of Iraq's export revenues. Repeated sabotage by those opposed to the American presence has reduced output to a level well below its potential. Despite this problem, oil production has been increasing by about 10 percent per year since the end of the second Gulf War.

Other Natural Resources

In addition to its vast oil reserves, Iraq has deposits of non-energy minerals. There are enough of some of these minerals that many are mined and sold in regional or global markets. The most mineral-rich region is the northern foothills and mountains, where mineralized belts of rock contain abundant quantities of coal, sulfur, lead, and zinc. Minor deposits of other minerals are found throughout the country, such as iron, gold, copper, silver, platinum, and uranium. Gypsum, phosphates, and salt are fairly abundant and are mined in central and western Iraq.

Although oil generates most of the national income, the majority of Iraq's labor force works at farming and livestock activities. These agricultural activities account for more than 10 percent of Iraq's gross domestic product (the value of all goods and services). Just like the oil sector, Iraq's agricultural production was impacted by the years of sanctions and war. These problems, together with a drought in the 1990s, brought food production in Iraq to a standstill. Much of the food currently consumed must be imported.

Iraq is a rarity in the Middle East, because its agricultural potential is far greater than what is now produced. Iraq is, in effect, underpopulated. It could easily feed more people than it does now. Nearly half of Iraq's land can be farmed, but only 13 percent of that amount is now plowed and planted. However, a great investment is needed to modernize the agricultural sector to make it more productive. The greatest potential for increased agricultural production exists where production is already highest: the irrigated lands of Mesopotamia, and the rain-fed arable land of northern Iraq.

Iraq's agricultural potential is fed by abundant water, one of the most important resources in the Middle East. A mighty flow of water courses through the famous Tigris and Euphrates rivers. This large supply of water, for Iraq's relatively small population, gives Iraqis one of the highest per-person volumes of water in the region.

Iraq has enormous economic potential. With its vast oil resources, population, and water supply, it could successfully develop many industries.

MANUFACTURING AND OTHER INDUSTRIES

Petroleum and natural gas products are refined on a limited basis, but manufacturing is not a well-developed industry in Iraq. Manufactured goods are largely limited to processed foods and beverages, textiles and clothing, metal products, furniture, footwear, cigarettes, and construction materials like bricks and concrete. The industrial heartland of central Iraq also has heavy industry (iron, steel, oil pipe, fertilizers) and petrochemical production.

Because of its large market and labor supply, Baghdad is the country's leading manufacturing center. Basra also has significant manufacturing activity, because of the nearby availability of oil and gas for energy and because of the Basra port facility, which serves as a center for imports and exports. After oil and gas in Iraq's north stimulated population and industrial growth, a third manufacturing area developed in the Kirkuk-Arbil-Mosul triangle. Important sectors of the service industry include government social services such as health and education, financial services, and personal services.

IMPORTS/EXPORTS AND REGIONAL TRADE

Foreign trade is an important part of economic stability. For major oil producing countries like Iraq, the export trade allows the country to sell its oil in international markets to make money. Because Iraq does not manufacture many products, it must import most manufactured goods. Iraq has been able to maintain a favorable balance of trade (exports exceed imports), because it can sell large quantities of valuable oil to offset the cost of the equipment, machinery, and spare parts that must be imported.

Petroleum sales account for almost all export earnings. Other exports are dates, raw wool, hides, and skins. Primary imports are machinery, transportation equipment, foodstuffs, and pharmaceuticals. Before the first Gulf War, Iraq's main trade partners were Brazil, Turkey, Japan, Germany, France, Italy, the United Kingdom, and the United States. After the Gulf War, Iraq's trading partners mainly included Russia, China, France, and Egypt. With the lifting of UN sanctions after the second Gulf War, Iraq is resuming trade relations with the international community, including with the United States. Iraq was granted observer status at the World Trade Organization (WTO) in 2004 and began working toward full member status.

In terms of human activity, Iraq is predominantly an agricultural country. Most of its farmland is around the Tigris and Euphrates rivers. Significant agricultural products include wheat, barley, and rice. Before the UN sanctions, Iraq accounted for a major share of the world trade in dates. Other

Dates are one of Iraq's primary exports; however, the UN sanctions of the early 1990s greatly affected the industry. Many Iraqis, including this man, rely on harvesting dates to make a living.

fruits produced include apples, figs, grapes, olives, oranges, pears, and pomegranates.

Raising livestock is an important occupation for Iraq's nomadic and seminomadic tribes. About 10 percent of Iraq's land is suitable for grazing. Iraq's livestock population includes mostly sheep, goats, and cattle. Camels are common in the driest areas, and poultry farms are found in more humid regions. The world-famous Arabian horse is extensively bred in Iraq, although demand for the breed has declined in recent years. Iraq also has a small fishing industry. Some of this industry involves saltwater fishing along Iraq's narrow coastal waters, but most of the annual harvest is freshwater fish from the rivers and lakes of Iraq.

AN ECONOMY IN TRANSITION

Iraq's economy has changed remarkably since the discovery of oil. Mostly traditional and agrarian (farm-based) a century ago, the modern Iraqi economy is now based on petroleum. Larger manufacturing industries also involve oil (refining and petrochemicals).

Beginning in 1980, the Iraqi economy was badly affected by four major factors: the war with Iran during the 1980s, an international oil surplus in the 1980s and 1990s, the economic sanctions imposed by the UN (after the invasion of Kuwait in 1990), and the Persian Gulf Wars in 1991 and 2003. The combined effect of all these factors was the destruction of Iraq's basic infrastructure (roads, bridges, power grids, and the like) and the country's financial bankruptcy.

Iraq's real gross domestic product (GDP)—that is, its GDP adjusted for inflation—fell by 75 percent from 1991 to 1999. In the 1990s, Iraq's GDP was estimated to be about what it was in the 1940s, before the oil boom and the modernization of the country. Many well-educated Iraqis fled, and the value of its national currency, the dinar, declined and drove prices upward. The government foolishly continued to finance its spending commitments by printing more money. This further devalued the currency and guaranteed that price increases would continue.

The 2003 military victory of the U.S.–led coalition (alliance) closed down much of Iraq's centralized economic administration. During the 2003–2005 postwar transition, Iraq's Interim Government created the many institutions needed to manage Iraq's economy. Only a small amount of Iraq's productive facilities and economic management buildings were damaged during the Gulf Wars. However, public looting, violent insurgent attacks, and sabotage against oil pipelines and other economic facilities have undermined efforts to rebuild the economy.

Oil remains the most important factor in future Iraqi growth, because so much of Iraq's global earnings are dependent on oil sales. Oil production has increased by about 10 percent per year for the first two years (2004–2005) after Gulf War II. Projected future growth in Iraq's oil production (60 percent growth from prewar 2002 until optimal production in 2010) would be enough to again make Iraq the second-largest producer in the Middle East.

Another key ingredient in rebuilding Iraq's economy is the reliable and enhanced generation of electricity. The 1991 and 2003 wars caused massive damage to power plants. During and between the wars, electricity was further limited, because the equipment used to generate and distribute electricity was getting old. Trade sanctions restricted spare parts and prevented the replacement of aging equipment. "Rolling blackouts"— shutting off electricity to different provinces and cities on a regular basis—was part of the daily routine for Iraqis. After the second Gulf War, many Iraqis had high hopes that the United States would soon replace the old electrical grid with a new system. The generation of electrical power has improved in most of the country, but attacks by insurgents against power-generating stations, and against workers trying to restore power, have slowed progress.

Despite the setbacks, new frontiers for trade and exchange have opened for Iraq. The country has been connected to the rest of the world through the Internet since 2004. Cellular phone service was available by 2005 in much of the country.

With trade sanctions erased, a growing number of international shipping companies have been operating out of Iraqi ports—from Basra to the Persian Gulf—since 2003. These ports were not badly damaged during the Gulf Wars. Also, the air freight of goods to Iraq has dramatically increased since 2003. Some of these shipments have been made by the U.S. or British air forces, or by chartered flights scheduled by international aid organizations. Two public airlines (Royal Jordanian and Iraqi Airways) now fly between Iraq and surrounding countries. Many more privately chartered flights (mostly from Jordan or Turkey) make the trip to Baghdad, Basra, or Arbil.

After almost 15 years of economic decline, the Iraqi economy is again surging. Real GDP growth was estimated at more than 50 percent in 2004–2005. The result of such high growth has also been very high inflation (rate of price increases), estimated at 25 percent in 2004. The creation of new jobs is growing in the country, though the unemployment rate is still relatively high (about 20 percent in 2005). A new Iraqi currency was created and began circulating in January 2004. The new Iraqi dinar replaced the old dinars that had Saddam Hussein's image on the banknotes.

CHAPTER

7

Living in Iraq Today

Iraq has changed considerably over the last century, with dramatic reforms occurring over the past few years. The economy is evolving and the political system has been completely overhauled. Ethnic and religious groups in Iraq are finding new ways of living with one another and creating new political charters that recognize their differences. The forces of globalization and social change are forcing young Iraqis, and their parents, to reassess values and decide what to adopt from the modern world and what to retain from the past. Many characteristics of Iraqi life remain essentially unchanged. All across Iraq, old traditions lend uniqueness to the timeless land of Mesopotamia.

STYLES OF DRESS

Traditional clothing in Iraq is similar to that found elsewhere in the Middle East. For women, these clothes include the *abaya* (ah-BAH-ya), a long dark robe worn as an outer cloak to cover the woman from head to ankle. Some abayas are very plain and some use texture, shade, or fringe to appear more stylish. Most are made from black cloth. Underneath the abaya, the woman may wear most anything—from stylish dresses to warm-up suits or blue jeans—because it is covered by the abaya and not seen in public. Some women who wear the abaya will also wear a veil over their face, so that only their eyes show. Veils are to be removed only in the home or in the presence of other women. The rules regarding clothing are meant to show modesty and not to suppress women. Many women who choose not to wear the abaya or veil might instead wear head scarves called *hijab* (HIH-jab) or *shayla* (SHAY-la). Traditionally, young girls begin to wear this conservative clothing after they begin their menstrual cycle.

There is no prevailing style for women in Iraq, and they are not required to wear the abaya, the veil, or the hijab. However, since the fall of the Baathist regime, many more women are wearing the hijab. Western-style clothing is also popular—including jeans, skirts, and T-shirts—especially among younger women. Some women in Iraq like the conservative clothing and some despise it. The style worn by a woman will depend on many things, including family tradition; position in society, whether she is Muslim or Christian; how strict her father or husband is; and personal preference.

Modesty in clothing also applies to men, so both men and women usually avoid tight clothing. Iraqi Arab men have traditionally worn a long-sleeve, ankle-length robe called a *thobe* (THOH-buh) or *galabiya* (jal-AH-bee-ya). Kurdish men commonly wear baggy pantaloons with a matching shirt and a cummerbund (cloth wrap) around the waist. For headgear, Kurdish men commonly wear a turban (tight twist of cloth around the head), while Arab men wear a *keffiyeh* (KEF-ee-ya), a flowing piece of cloth covering the head and held in

Since the fall of the Baathist regime in 2003, Western-style clothing has become popular among many Iraqis. Here, two Baghdad State University students—one wearing the traditional *hijab*, or head scarf, and the other wearing Western clothing—converse at the entrance to the school.

place by a thick cord. These head coverings may be worn with traditional clothing or with Western-style pants and shirts. Among Iraqi businessmen and professionals, Western-style suits are very common. Jeans and T-shirts, preferably with something written on it in English, are very popular among young Iraqi males.

Styles of dress are thoroughly mixed in city and country, though certain trends are noticeable by region and by gender. Generally speaking, traditional styles of dress are more common in villages and rural areas, while Western styles of dress dominate clothing styles in the cities. Mature women are more likely to wear traditional styles of dress. Men, children, and teens have more commonly adopted Western clothing.

FAMILY LIFE AND GENDER ROLES

Life in Iraq revolves around family and extended kinship groups. The extended family is the basic social unit that regulates behavior, friendships, marriage, occupations, and political activity. The family remains the primary focus of loyalty and personal identity. A person's honor and dignity are greatly valued. Iraqis are generous and loyal people. They are very polite to friends and kind to strangers.

In traditional Iraq (especially in rural areas), the extended family—grandparents, parents, children, uncles, aunts, and cousins—all live together. Family members sometimes live separately while sharing the values and functions of an extended family, such as helping one another and respecting the wisdom of the older generation. Authority within the family is determined by seniority and by gender. The father (in theory) is the disciplinarian and authority figure—the head of the family.

A father usually decides what education his children will receive, what occupations his sons will enter, whether or not his daughters will have an occupation, and—usually in consultation with his wife—whom his children will marry. A person's character, background, and financial position are all taken into account for marriage decisions. In traditional Iraqi families, especially in rural areas, marriage between cousins is common. This ensures that money and property will remain in the family. In cities, especially among more educated families, young people increasingly choose their own partners, though parents must still approve of the choice. Most Iraqi families are large, with women generally having between five and six children. Urban families are usually smaller (three or four children) than those living in the country.

Women have traditionally been discouraged from finding employment and living independent lives. In rural areas, they may rarely leave the house except to visit friends. However, with so many wars fought in Iraq in recent decades, many men have been killed. This has led to a shortage of labor, and forced some women to find employment to help support the family. With women filling many of the jobs previously held by men, the traditional view that a wife's place is in the home is no longer strictly followed. Most clerical positions are now filled by women. They also work as supervisors, doctors, law enforcement officers, and elected government officials. Women are playing a visible and important role in the rebuilding process since the 2003 conflict.

Although women have joined the workforce, and have the same voting privileges as men, there are still clearly defined roles for each in Iraqi society. Outside the home, men and women are segregated. When friends get together, men and women usually divide into separate groups. It is considered improper for an unmarried man and woman to be alone with one another together, though this may be overlooked in the cities where men and women commonly work together.

SOCIAL SERVICES AND EDUCATION

There was a massive expansion in social services in Iraq during the 1980s. Many housing developments were completed, schools were opened in every village, and hospitals and clinics were set up throughout the country. A major health campaign was launched. The number of doctors and dentists doubled, and the number of pharmacists increased greatly.

One of the government's most successful development programs is education. Almost every village in Iraq has at least an elementary school. Every town has a secondary school, although rural schools are often built of mud brick and have tin roofs. Education is provided free by the state. Six years of primary education are compulsory, although many children do not attend because they must work to support the family. The literacy rate—percent of the population that can read and write—averages about 40 percent among those 15 and older. More than twice as many men (56 percent) are literate than women (24).

The origins of the Iraqi educational system are found in the traditional Koranic schools—religious institutions associated with mosques. Throughout the centuries, these schools have provided a basic education; scriptures are memorized and the interpretations given by religious instructors (*mullahs*) is never questioned. Even in modern Iraq, most students in schools and colleges concentrate on memorizing facts. They are taught to believe that the teacher is always right. A high value is placed on education, and a degree or diploma is a valued passport to a good job and improved salary. After the 2003 conflict and the removal of Saddam Hussein, school textbooks in Iraq were revised. Images of Saddam and the Baath Party were removed. Much of the propaganda and distortions of historical events were removed. Concepts of democracy and tolerance have entered textbooks, though sensitive issues like religion and the U.S. invasion are still not settled.

Iraq has a distinguished history of higher education and maintains 22 colleges and universities. Education is given a high priority by the Iraqi government. The government recognizes that a literate and skilled population is essential if Iraq is to continue its social progress and its industrial and technological advancement. During the lost years of 1980 to 2003, much of the national income was diverted from education to support the war efforts, and UN sanctions prevented new technology from being imported to Iraq. As a result, one of the finest university systems in the Middle East lost its edge. Programs were poorly funded and poorly equipped. University classrooms and faculty research both suffered from loss of contact with the outside world. Since 2004, U.S. and international efforts to help rebuild Iraqi higher education have brought new technologies and programs into Iraqi universities. Today, the Iraqi system of higher education is once again moving forward.

HEALTH AND MEDICINE

The Iraqi government has tried to improve health standards, and had good medical facilities until the 1990s. In September

1985, Iraq began the first stage of a national campaign to vaccinate its schoolchildren against tetanus, diphtheria, whooping cough, poliomyelitis, tuberculosis, measles, and German measles. Substantial progress also has been made in controlling malaria. Improvements in flood control, water supply, and sewage systems improved sanitation and made dreadful epidemics (in which thousands of people died) a thing of the past. Government health education campaigns improved people's understanding of the importance of hygiene. As with other sectors of society, the campaign to improve the health of Iraqi citizens was affected by wars and sanctions, and much progress was lost.

Since 1990, Iraq's health standards have declined. Diseases, poor sanitary conditions (especially in the water supply), and lack of food and medicines have all taken their toll. In 2001, life expectancy at birth was 58 for Iraqi males and 60 for females, both about 20 years short of the same figures for the United States. The infant death rate was approximately 92 per 1,000 live births. Most medical facilities did not have enough supplies, and they needed repairs and modernization.

Since 2003, international aid agencies working with Iraqis have rehabilitated water treatment plants and replaced leaking water pipes. They have introduced new technologies into hospitals and clinics, greatly expanded the availability of medicines, and distributed food to a malnourished population. As a result, the 2006 estimated life expectancy has climbed 10 years higher since 2001. It is now 68 for males and 70 for females, and the infant death rate (50 per 1,000 live births) is about half what it was in 2001.

ROADS AND TRANSPORTATION

Neither roads nor railroad systems were ever well developed in Iraq. The country has railroad connections (through Syria) with Turkey and Europe. The Iraqi state railway network has about 1,500 miles (2,430 kilometers) of track, but the system is poorly planned and is seldom used for passenger traffic. Plans

Iraq's transportation infrastructure has always been ill-suited to handle its large population. Although plans are in the works to add several thousand miles of track to its railroad system, the country has had a difficult time maintaining its network of trains, many of which are falling apart and travel at very slow speeds.

have been developed to add another 2,000 miles (3,225 kilometers) of tracks that would connect Iraq's major cities.

In a virtually landlocked country such as Iraq, good roadways are very important. Iraq has about 30,000 miles (48,000 kilometers) of roads, of which about 25,000 miles (40,000 kilometers) are paved. A few major four-lane highways surround Baghdad, run south to Basra and west to the Jordanian border, and connect Kirkuk and Sulaymaniyah in the Kurdish region. Before the devastation of the recent wars, the highways were strained by Iraq's growth. Wars, sanctions, and a soured economy reduced traffic, but this trend is being reversed in the new postwar era. Dozens of bridges and road junctions destroyed in the Gulf Wars were repaired after 2003. Most Iraqis still can't afford cars, so hitchhiking and public transport are common means of travel. However, thousands of new and used cars have been flooding into the country, some through Jordan but mostly through Kuwait. For those who can afford a vehicle, gasoline is very cheap, costing less than U.S. 10 cents per gallon in 2004. The great crush of new traffic is starting to overwhelm the highways around the major cities (especially Baghdad), and long traffic delays during peak travel periods have been common since 2004. There are plans for upgrading and expanding the national highway system.

Iraq has developed several port facilities—for oil export and general ship cargo—by flooding areas of the lower Shatt al-Arab waterway. All of Iraq's ports are located along the narrow strip of water between Basra and the Persian Gulf. The narrowness of Iraq's seacoast restricts the country's ports to this small area. Small river steamers are able to navigate the Tigris River from Basra to Baghdad.

Oil pipelines carry Iraq's most valuable resource between the oil-producing areas around Basra (south) and Kirkuk (north). In addition to shipping its oil out through the Persian Gulf waterway, pipelines carry Iraqi oil to international markets through Saudi Arabia, Jordan, and Turkey. These alternate routes were used heavily by Iraq during the Iran-Iraq War, after Iran captured the Shatt al-Arab waterway and closed off Iraq's ports. International sanctions closed these oil routes during and between the Gulf Wars, but they were again opened in 2003 to ship Iraqi oil to help fund reconstruction programs.

International airports serve Baghdad and Basra, although during times of war or other national crises the government has banned international travel. Iraqi Airways, Iraq's national air carrier, resumed international flights in 2004 after 14 years of being grounded by war and sanctions. The airline began with scheduled flights to Jordan and Syria twice a week. Chartered flights from Jordan and Turkey are now common.

SPORT AND LEISURE

Soccer ("football" to Iraqis) is the most popular sport in the world and the favorite sport of Iraqis. The games in Baghdad draw thousands of loud and supportive fans. Iraq is a member of the Asian Football Confederation (AFC), and the country competes every year in the Asian Nations Cup. There is growing interest in basketball, volleyball, boxing, and wrestling. During the years of wars and sanctions, international travel to or from Iraq was greatly reduced. This restricted the opportunities for Iraqi athletes to compete in the international arena.

Iraqis enjoy fishing, swimming, and boating in the Tigris and Euphrates rivers, and in the Persian Gulf. These activities are mostly limited to the warmer months in central and northern Iraq. In warmer southern Iraq, Iraqis enjoy water sports for most of the year. Many Iraqis enjoy hiking and camping in the cooler mountains of northern Iraq. A small ski area used to operate in the higher mountains for the few Iraqis who pursue this sport. The facility was closed during the wars, but is expected to reopen in the future.

TELEVISION, THE INTERNET, AND CELL PHONES

In 1988, Iraqi radio and television stations came under central government control (Iraqi Broadcasting and Television Establishment, or Baghdad Television). Radio service was broadcast mainly in Arabic, but also (from Kirkuk) in Kurdish, Turkomen, and Assyrian. Television stations were located in major cities. Baghdad Television had two program networks (two channels). Programs broadcast by Iraqi radio and television were tightly controlled by the central government. Iraqis could get little information about the outside world from these sources, but satellite television dishes are now starting to appear in the country.

As bombs fell during the Gulf Wars, Iraqis could not head for the Internet to connect with loved ones or pass on information to relatives abroad. Although e-mail is increasingly used around the world as a grassroots communications link, Iraq had no Internet systems or services. Sources of open information—like the World Wide Web—were forbidden under the government of Saddam Hussein. The paranoid central government refused to open Iraqi society to anything that it could not control. Also, computers were prohibited by United Nations sanctions, and phone lines damaged in the 1991 Gulf War had not been replaced. A few Internet portals opened in autonomous Kurdish regions of Iraq in the 1990s. Most of the country, including Baghdad, gained access to the Internet during spring and summer of 2004. Most Iraqis still do not have access to computers, but they are becoming increasingly common in universities and at public "Internet cafes" in the cities.

The 2003 war severely disrupted telecommunications in Iraq, but international aid groups and businesses have been repairing the landlines and constructing mobile and satellite telephone facilities. Cellular phone service was first introduced in 2004 and cell phones are now common across much of the country.

Iraq Looks Ahead

I raqis are recovering from their misfortune. They are generally hopeful, even in the midst of change and turmoil. Iraqis are well educated, resourceful, and have enormous quantities of oil to fund their future plans. Widespread voter participation indicates that Iraq has taken an important first step toward democracy and self-governance. When the current hurdles are cleared—by improving security and electing politicians to implement the new government—the future of Iraq could be very bright. But the path is not clear; several challenges block the road to recovery.

CHALLENGE 1: FEDERALISM

The new Iraqi constitution, completed in August 2005 and approved by the Iraqi people in October of that year, promotes the principles of democracy and a federal system for Iraq. In a federal system, the governments in each province (or state) are elected locally and send representatives to the National Assembly (central government). This is much like the U.S. system where states have their own governments, and the states send representatives to the central government to look after their interests. This federal system allows the different groups in Iraq—Sunni, Shia, Kurd, and other ethnic minorities—to maintain regional control over their territory. It also allows the regions to decide how much power to give to the central government.

So why is federalism a "challenge"? The new federal constitution has been strongly supported by the Shia and Kurdish populations of Iraq—the groups that were historically dominated by the minority Sunni Arab population. However, most Sunni Arabs have not been happy with the situation. Federalism will not work if members of the federation do not accept the system. Southern U.S. states once tried to leave the federation of the United States of America when they no longer accepted the authority of the federal government. The United States fought a civil war in the 1860s to keep these states from leaving the federation. Will a majority of Sunni Arabs willingly join the federation, or will a civil war be needed in Iraq to work out these differences?

CHALLENGE 2: SUNNI FRUSTRATION

Since Islam first came to Iraq in the seventh century (except for very brief periods of Persian control), Sunni Muslims have been the political leaders of the territory—including the Umayyads, Abbasids, Seljuk and Ottomans Turks, Kings Faisal and Ghazi, and the Baathist leadership of the Saddam Hussein government. All of these governments had Sunnis (Sunni Turks and Sunni Arabs) controlling other people, so many Sunnis view themselves as the natural leaders of the broader Mesopotamian region.

In 1936, Iraq moved toward a pan-Arab alliance with the other Sunni governments of the Arab World. Iraq experienced its first military coup d'état in 1936, when the army overthrew the pan-Arab Sunni government. The leaders of the coup included a Kurdish general and a Shia politician, representing the groups (Kurd and Shia Arab) most opposed to Pan-Arabism. Interestingly, these two groups have allied themselves again in this recent round of state-making. The Kurds and the Shia Arabs—groups that were persecuted under the monarchies and dictatorships of Iraq—have found common ground on a number of issues. Sunni Arabs now feel threatened by these changes.

A large number of Sunni Arabs voted against the 2005 constitution, because the new system awards representation in government on the basis of population. The Sunni Arabs have only half the population of Shia Arabs in Iraq, and are only a bit more numerous than the Kurds. A democratic and federal Iraq will have many more Shia and Kurd than Sunni representatives, thereby diminishing Sunni Arab control over the country. This has left many Sunnis feeling marginalized and frustrated. Some Sunnis have become angry. Some have acted on these feelings by joining the insurgency that seeks to kill U.S. soldiers, disrupt the new government, and prevent the federal system from taking root.

Sunni disenchantment must be reversed by empowering the Sunnis. The Shias and Kurds in government must share power with Sunni Arabs and make it clear that a federal Iraq is not an anti-Sunni Iraq. Sunnis may no longer control the instruments of power, but through the federal political process they can still work to shape an Iraq that meets their needs and interests. After boycotting January 2005 elections in protest, the Sunnis finally joined the political process and turned to the ballot box to voice their concerns in elections held in October and December 2005.

CHALLENGE 3: KURDISTAN

In the referendum to approve the new constitution in October 2005, the Kurdish population of Iraq overwhelmingly voted in

Iraq's Kurdish population overwhelmingly supports a unified Iraq; however, maintaining their cultural identity is also very important to them. To that end, many Kurdish children, such as these fourth-grade students in the village of Hwana, spend the majority of their time learning Kurdish, not Arabic.

favor of the document. In the three major Kurdish provinces of Iraq, 99 percent of voters supported the federal constitution. This suggests that Iraq's Kurds largely approve of federalism and wish to live with the Arabs in a unified Iraq. The situation, in reality, is more complex.

Most Kurds would prefer to create a new independent country of Kurdistan. This has been a dream of the Kurdish people in Turkey, Syria, Iraq, and Iran since the Ottoman Empire broke up almost a century ago. Many Kurdish intellectuals have written new books on the advantages of independence; although, Kurdish politicians debate the subject more often between themselves than with members of the international community. For it is the international community, with its complex network of alliances, that bars the way to independence for the Kurds.

Turkey is most strongly opposed to Kurdish independence. If an independent Kurdistan ever existed, the large Kurdish population in eastern Turkey might try to join the new country. This would cause civil war in Turkey. The Turks have struggled against their own Kurdish rebels over this very issue before. Turkey is a strong ally of the United States. The United States does not want to anger Turkey by encouraging Kurdish independence. Therefore, the United States has made it clear that it wishes Iraq's Kurds to live in a united Iraq.

The Kurds owe their present freedoms and new influence in the Iraqi government to the United States. It was the United States that helped protect their territory from a vengeful Saddam Hussein in the 1990s, and then removed him from power in 2003. So the Kurds do not want to anger the United States, which they view as a very good and trusted friend. Also, surrounding Arab states do not want to see the Arab state of Iraq break apart with the departure of the Kurds. Many of these Arab states are friends of the United States. Consequently, the Kurds do not wish to hurt their friendship with the United States by breaking away and angering America's friends in the region. So the Kurds, instead, work to secure greater control over their affairs (autonomy) within a democratic and federal Iraq. To most Kurds, this is not as good as complete independence, but it is much better than the old Arab dictatorship that persecuted and murdered many Kurdish people.

The Kurds have agreed to federalism for now. A major challenge for the future—for the integrity of Iraq—will be to keep the Kurds in Iraq. Alliances and friendships change over time. No one knows how these changes will affect the Kurdish desire for independence in the future.

CHALLENGE 4: ISLAMIC OR SECULAR PATH?

As the new Iraqi Constitution took shape, there were many debates in government, and among ordinary Iraqis, over the

Prior to the acceptance of Iraq's constitution in October 2005, many Iraqi groups preferred a government that supported the separation of church and state. However, largely due to Shia influence, Iraq's constitution is based on a combination of civil (secular) and Islamic law.

role that Islam should play in the new government and its constitution. Most Shia Arabs want Islam to be enshrined as a guiding principle for new laws in Iraq. However, Shia Arabs differ over how prominent this role should be. Some clearly prefer a conservative Islamic state, like Iran's Islamic theocracy (church and state together in one system). Some Shias prefer a government guided by sharia (Islamic law), but not a strict, fundamentalist government. The Kurds want a clear separation of church and state and are the biggest supporters of a secular (nonreligious) form of government. Sunni views on the matter of religion in government have been mixed.

The new constitution approved by the Iraqi people in 2005 is based on a combination of civil (secular) and Islamic law. This compromise works for now and may continue to work. However, the country's majority Shia population is the group most in favor of a greater role for Islam in government. In the new federal system, the Shias have more influence over the shaping of laws, because of their larger population and corresponding greater numbers in government. If the Shias use this numeric advantage to gradually create a more fundamentalist (and less secular) government, the Kurds may wish to leave the federation. With the Kurds gone, the Sunni-Shia balance would be shifted further in favor of the Shias. This is because the Kurds—in terms of their religion—are mostly Sunni Muslim. With the Kurds part of a united Iraq, the Sunni-Shia balance would be approximately 40 percent to 60 percent. With the Kurdish portion of Iraq's Sunni Muslims out of the picture, the remaining Muslim population shifts to about 25 percent Sunni and 75 percent Shia Muslim. Sunni Arabs would feel even more marginalized under such a system and would likely follow the Kurds by abandoning the federation.

In short, if the Sunni Kurds leave the federation, so, too, may the Sunni Arabs. Therefore, whether Iraq follows a secular or a more Islamist path will play a role in whether the future Iraqi state stays together or breaks up.

CHALLENGE 5: INSURGENCY

The news from Iraq is both good and bad. On the negative side, insurgents use ambushes and roadside bombs to kill U.S. troops and kidnap and murder Iraqi politicians and "collaborators." This degraded security environment slows reconstruction and the return to normal life in Iraq. Political and social systems are changing rapidly. All of this creates constant tension and an uncertain future.

But there is a great deal of good news, too, much of which, unfortunately, is rarely covered by the American media. Improved electricity generation and cleaner water supplies allow industry to grow and allow people to live more normal and healthy lives. Expanding oil production and oil exports earn much money to help Iraq rebuild itself. Religious and political freedoms, not possible under the old government, are now enjoyed by Iraqis. Notable improvements to schools—both structural and curricular—are modernizing Iraqi public education. New facilities and programs in universities provide access to new technology. These changes are helping to bring Iraq into the global society of the twenty-first century.

Some Iraqis (as well as many foreign fighters) who object to the U.S. occupation and the new political system are trying to destabilize Iraq. This insurgency presents the greatest challenge of all. Iraq has great potential because of its oil, water, and other resources. It has an educated and skilled population and economic growth has begun. A new political era in a new democratic and federal Iraq has just dawned in old Mesopotamia, yet many Iraqi people today endure great hardships.

More jobs are being created, but the economy of Iraq was so damaged during events of the past 25 years that it will take more than a quick fix to return the country to the prosperity it experienced prior to 1980. Steady progress may continue. However, only after the political situation has stabilized and a majority of Sunni Arabs support the new political process will the problem of domestic security be stabilized. If security is achieved, the country finally will be able to continue work toward the realization of its vast natural and human resource potential.

Facts at a Glance

Physical Geography

Location Middle East, east of Syria and Jordan, bordering the Persian Gulf between Iran and Kuwait; about the size of California

Area Total: 168,756 square miles (437,072 square kilometers); *land:* 166,862 square miles (432,162 square kilometers); *water:* 1,896 square miles (4,910 square kilometers)

Climate and Ecosystem Mostly desert; mild to cool winters with dry, hot, cloudless summers; northern mountainous regions along Iranian and Turkish borders experience cold winters with occasionally heavy snows

Terrain Stony, desert plains in dry western Iraq; broad alluvial (river deposited) plains in Mesopotamia; marshes along the Iranian border in the south with large flooded areas; hills in the northeast with high mountains along the borders with Iran and Turkey

Elevation Extremes Lowest point is the Persian Gulf (sea level); highest point is an unnamed peak, 11,847 feet (3,611 meters)

Land Use Arable land, 13.12%; permanent crops, 0.61%; other, 86.27% (2005)

Irrigated Land 13,610 square miles (35,250 square kilometers) (2003)

Natural Hazards Dust storms, sandstorms, floods

Environmental Issues Most of the inhabited marsh areas east of Nasiriyah have been drained by the government, forcing the inhabitants, known as Marsh Arabs, to be displaced—the destruction of this natural habitat has also threatened the area's wildlife populations; inadequate supplies of potable water; air and water pollution; soil degradation (salination) and erosion; desertification

People

Population 26,783,383 (July 2006 est.); males, 13,551,602 (2006 est.); females, 13,231,781 (2006 est.)

Population Density 154 people per square mile (59 per square kilometer)

Population Growth Rate 2.66% (2006 est.)

Net Migration Rate 0.00 migrant(s)/1,000 population (2006 est.)

Fertility Rate 4.18 children born/woman (2006 est.)

Life Expectancy at Birth	Total population: 69.01 years; male, 67.76 years; female, 70.31 years (2006 est.)
Median Age	19.7 years; male, 19.6 years; female, 19.8 years (2006 est.)
Ethnic Groups	Arab, 75%–80%; Kurdish, 15%–20%, Turkoman, Assyrian, or other, 5%
Religions	Muslim, 97% (Shia, 60%–65%, Sunni, 32%–37%); Christian or other, 3%
Literacy	(age 15 and over can read and write) Total population: 40.4%; male, 55.9%; female, 24.4% (2003 est.)

Economy

Currency	New Iraqi dinar (NID) as of January 2004
GDP Purchasing Power Parity (PPP)	$94.1 billion (2005 est.)
GDP Per Capita (PPP)	$3,400 (2005 est.)
Labor Force	7.4 million (2004 est.)
Unemployment	25 to 30% (2005 est.)
Labor Force by Occupation	Agriculture, NA%; industry, NA%; services, NA%
Industries	Petroleum, chemicals, textiles, leather, construction materials, food processing, fertilizer, metal fabrication/processing
Exports	$17.78 billion (2004 est.)
Imports	$19.57 billion (2004 est.)
Leading Trade Partners	*Exports*: U.S., 51.9%; Spain, 7.3%; Japan, 6.6%; Italy, 5.7%; Canada, 5.2% (2004) *Imports*: Syria, 22.9%; Turkey, 19.5%; U.S., 9.2%; Jordan, 6.7%; Germany, 4.9% (2004)
Export Commodities	Crude oil (83.9%), crude materials excluding fuels (8.0%), food and live animals (5.0%)
Import Commodities	Food, medicine, manufactures
Transportation	*Roadways*: 28,304 miles (45,550 kilometers); paved, 23,861 miles (38,399 kilometers); unpaved, 4,444 miles (7,151 kilometers) (1999); *Airports:* 111–78 with paved runways (2005); *Waterways:* 3,280 miles (5,279 kilometers)–primarily Euphrates River 1,749 miles (2,815 kilometers) and Tigris River 1,180 miles (1,899 kilometers) (2004)

Government

Country Name	Conventional long form: Republic of Iraq; Conventional short form: Iraq; Local long form: Al Jumhuriyah al Iraqiyah; Local short form: Al Iraq

Capital City	Baghdad
Type of Government	Transitional democracy
Head of Government	Nouri al-Maliki was named prime minister-designate on April 21, 2006. He is the first prime minister appointed under the terms of the new constitution.
Independence	October 3, 1932 (from League of Nations mandate under British administration); On June 28, 2004, the Coalition Provisional Authority transferred sovereignty to the Iraqi Interim Government
Administrative Divisions	18 governorates (muhafazat, singular—muhafazah)

Communications

TV Stations	21 (2004)
Phones	(including cellular): 1,608,200 (2004)
Internet Users	36,000 (2005)

* Source: *CIA-The World Factbook* (2006)

B.C.

4000 The city of Sumer is built in Mesopotamia, at the mouth of the Euphrates River on the Persian Gulf; it is the model for all the later city-states of the Middle East and the Mediterranean world.

3000 Centered around their original city-state of Assur, in northern Iraq, the Assyrians emerge as a regional power.

1700 Under Hammurabi, the city of Babylon (south of Baghdad) becomes the capital of the new Babylonian Empire; Hammurabi writes the first legal code.

1116 The Assyrian Empire revives and reaches its greatest extent.

616 Assyrian power finally ends and a new Babylonian Empire rises.

A.D.

661 The Islamic world falls under the leadership of the Umayyad Dynasty; their capital is in Damascus but they control most of Iraq.

763 Baghdad is established as the capital of the new Islamic Abbasid Empire.

1055 Seljuk Turks conquer Baghdad.

1258 The Mongols destroy Baghdad.

1533–1547 Iraq becomes part of the Ottoman Empire.

1918 British troops drive remaining Turkish troops from Iraq, taking possession of the oil fields around Mosul.

1932 Iraq becomes independent from British rule; Faisal I is first king.

1958 King Faisal is killed in a military coup (seizure of power), and the Hashemite Kingdom is replaced by a military government with Abdel Karim Kassem as the new prime minister.

1961 The Kurdish minority concentrated in northwestern Iraq starts a revolt.

1963 Members of the Baath Party come to power.

1970 New Iraqi constitution enacted; Arabs and Kurds named as co-nationalities of a binational Iraq; Iraq nationalizes the oil industry, most of which was owned and operated by British companies.

1979 Saddam Hussein becomes the leader of the Baath Party; by rules of the 1970 constitution, this makes him president of Iraq.

1990	National Assembly names Saddam Hussein "President for Life"; historic territorial claims, and disputes over war debts and oil deposits lead to an Iraqi invasion and occupation of Kuwait (August 4).
1991	Iraq is invaded and devastated by a massive military attack by an international coalition (January and February); Kuwait is liberated; outlying Kurdish and Shia areas of Iraq are occupied by Western troops.
1990s	Saddam Hussein and the Baathist government remain in power; United Nations sponsored economic sanctions prevent Iraq from exporting much oil and blockade all except bare essentials (food and medicine) from being shipped into Iraq; Iraq interferes with UN weapons inspectors looking for illegal weapons, but international support for another military attack is lacking.
2000	The U.S. Department of State places Iraq on its list of nations that sponsor terrorism.
2001	The terrorist attacks of September 11 in the United States bring Iraq under scrutiny for its possible involvement in global terrorism and place the country on the list of potential future targets in the war on terrorism.
2003	The United States, with British and other allies, launches a "shock and awe" air bombardment of Iraq, followed by massive invasion of the country from the north and south; Iraq is occupied by U.S. and British troops; Saddam Hussein is removed from power and the Baath Party is disbanded; Iraq is controlled by the U.S.–administered Coalition Provision Authority (CPA).
2004	Control of Iraq is transferred to the Iraqi Interim Government (IIG); U.S. and British keep military forces in Iraq to help the new Iraqi police and army maintain internal security.
2005	Democratic elections held January 2005 for a Transitional National Assembly (TNA)—the first real democratic elections in Iraq's history; the TNA drafts the permanent Iraqi Constitution, which is approved by more than 75 percent of Iraqi voters in an October referendum; elections for new Iraqi government held December 2005.

Arnov, Anthony, and Ali Abunimah. *Iraq under Siege: The Deadly Impact of Sanctions and War.* Cambridge, Mass.: South End Press, 2000.

Central Intelligence Agency. *CIA—The World Fact Book, Iraq.* *www.cia.gov/cia/publications/factbook (current).*

Danchev, Alex, and John MacMillan, eds. *The Iraq War and Democratic Politics.* New York: Routledge, 2005.

Dodge, Toby. *Inventing Iraq: The Failure of Nation Building and a History Denied.* New York: Columbia University Press, 2003.

Embassy of Saudi Arabia. *Understanding Islam and the Muslims.* Washington, D.C.: The Embassy of Saudi Arabia, 1989.

Fromkin, David. *A Peace To End All Peace: Creating the Modern Middle East, 1914–1922.* New York: Henry Holt, 1989.

Held, Colbert C. *Middle East Patterns: Places, Peoples, and Politics.* Boulder, Colo.: Westview Press, 2006.

Hourani, Albert, Phillip Khoury, and Mary Wilson, eds. *The Modern Middle East: A Reader.* Berkeley, Calif.: University of California Press, 1994.

Lewis, Bernard. *The Middle East: A Brief History of the Last 2,000 Years.* New York: Scribner, 1996.

Marr, Phebe. *The Modern History of Iraq.* Boulder, Colo.: Westview Press, 1985.

Metz, Helen Chapin. *Iraq: A Country Study.* Washington, D.C.: U.S. Government Printing Office, 1990.

Payne, Robert. *The History of Islam.* New York: Barnes and Noble, 1995.

Spencer, William. *Global Studies: The Middle East (Iraq Country Report).* Dubuque, Iowa: 2004.

United States Department of State—*Background Notes on Iraq.* *http://www.state.gov/r/pa/ei/bgn/6804.htm (current).*

Further Reading

Britton, Tamara L. *Iraq*. Edina, Minn.: ABDO Publishing Company, 2000.

Dudley, William, ed. *Iraq: Opposing Viewpoints*. New York: Greenhaven Press, 2004.

Hassig, Susan M. *Cultures of the World: Iraq*. New York: Marshall Cavendish, 1995.

King, John. *A Family from Iraq*. Milwaukee, Wisc.: Raintree Publishers, 1997.

Malinowski, Jon C. *Iraq: Geographic Perspectives*. Guilford, Conn.: McGraw-Hill, 2004.

Richie, Jason. *Iraq and the Fall of Saddam Hussein*. Minneapolis, Minn.: The Oliver Press, 2003.

Service, Pamela F. *Mesopotamia: Cultures of the Past*. Ipswich, Mass.: Marshall Vacendish Corporation, 1999.

Spencer, William. *Iraq: Old Land, New Nation in Conflict*. Breckenridge, Colo.: Twenty First Century Books, 2000.

Taus-Bolstad, Stacy. *Iraq in Pictures*. Minneapolis, Minn.: Lerner Publications, 2004.

Whitcraft, Melissa. *The Tigris Euphrates Rivers*. New York: Scholastic Library Publishing, 1999.

Web sites

Frontline: The Gulf War
   http://www-c.pbs.org/wgbh/pages/frontline/gulf/

The Iraq Foundation: Promoting Democracy in Iraq
   http://www.iraqfoundation.org/

Library of Congress: Iraq, A Country Study
   http://lcweb2.loc.gov/frd/cs/iqtoc.html

Interactive Guide to Assyria, Babylonia and Sumer
   http://www.mesopotamia.co.uk/

Index

Index

Index

Picture Credits

page:

DALE LIGHTFOOT is professor and head of the Department of Geography at Oklahoma State University. Dr. Lightfoot is a specialist on the Middle East and has taught geography at the university level for nearly two decades. He has traveled through every country in the Middle East, including research trips in Morocco, Jordan, Syria, and Yemen. During 2004–2005, Lightfoot traveled around much of Iraq. He worked closely with Iraqi university professors and government ministries through programs to rebuild Iraqi higher education.

Series editor **CHARLES F. GRITZNER** is distinguished professor of geography at South Dakota State University in Brookings. He is now in his fifth decade of college teaching, research, and writing. In addition to teaching, he enjoys writing, working with teachers, and sharing his love of geography with readers. As the series editor for Chelsea House's MODERN WORLD CULTURES and MODERN WORLD NATIONS series, he has a wonderful opportunity to combine each of these hobbies. Gritzner has served as both president and executive director of the National Council for Geographic Education and has received the Council's highest honor, the George J. Miller Award for Distinguished Service to Geographic Education.